I0493625

Nepal Smiles Again: a Collection of Portraits

Manoj Pandey

Copyright © 2016 Manoj Pandey
Cover Design by Robert Markey

ISBN 978-1536929881

This photobook is a product of rigorous field visits and discussions with the survivors of the Nepal earthquake of April, 2015. Hence, I would like to dedicate this compilation to the survivors who are resilient and have coped with the aftermath of the disaster. Further, this book wouldn't have been published without the support of Robert Markey, artist from United States of America, and his wife Julie Orfirer. They deserve a deep sense of respect.

Foreword

I met Manoj in December of 2014 at a ten-day conflict resolution training session in Kathmandu. Just a few months later, in April, the terrible earthquake happened. Since I had just been there, and had some new friends there, I spent time making sure all my friends were safe, and then did a fundraiser to help with the response. All the photos were difficult to look at because of such destruction.

Just a few months later I saw some photographs of people laughing that Manoj put up on his website. It was so wonderful to see these after all the photos of devastation. Manoj then put together a file of the photos with descriptions and sent it to me. When I looked at this I thought that it should be published as a book. I had done three books with CreateSpace before, and I told him that I could do the technical aspects and we can get it published. So here is the amazing work by Manoj.

Robert Markey

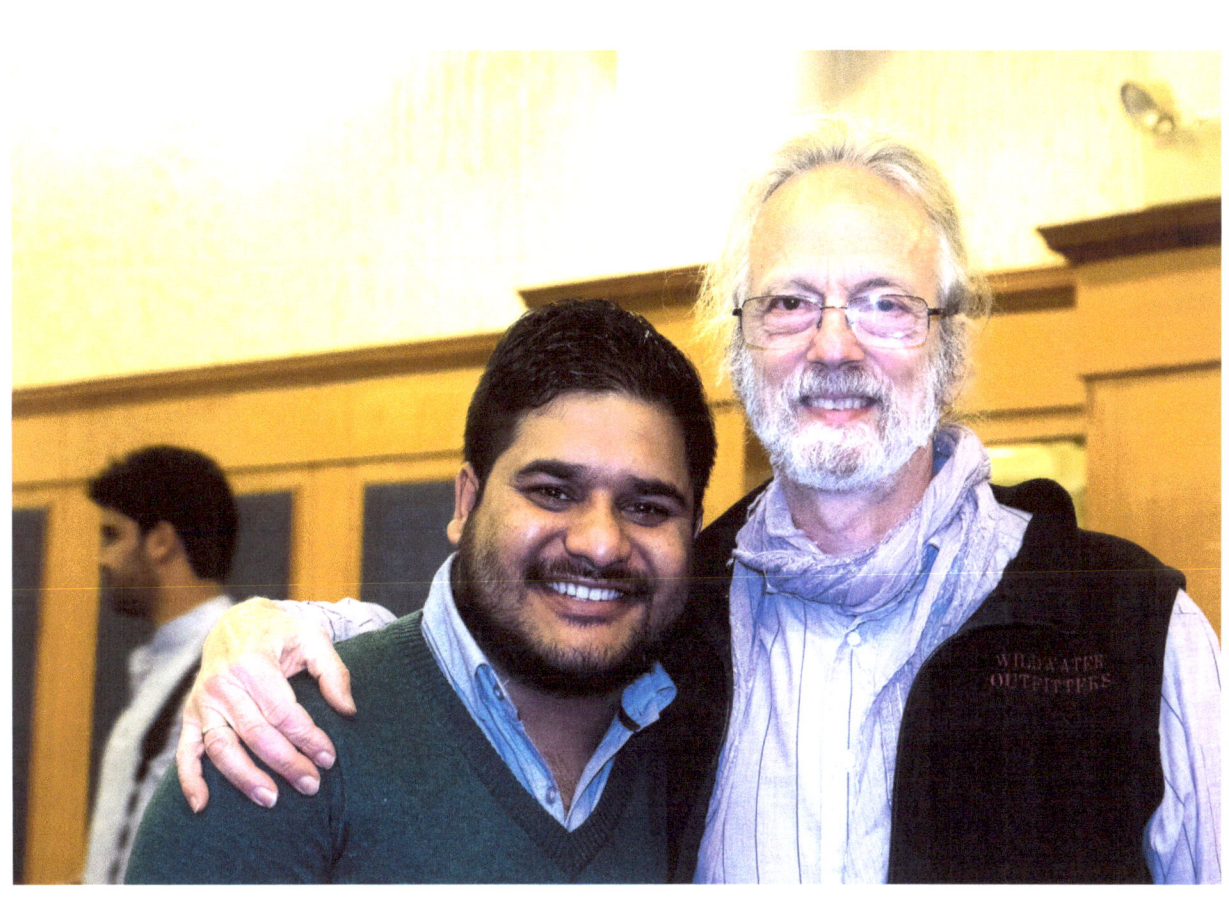

Nepal Smiles Again:
A Collection of Portraits

After decades of political mayhem, when it finally looked like Nepal was ready to head on the right track, nature struck a fatal blow—a devastating earthquake sent people across the nation in a frenzy. Many lost their lives, many lost all they could call their own, and for those who survived there were too many pieces to pick up. What followed for most of the year came in the form of aftershocks with fear mounting with each one. Displaced, hurt and panic-stricken, hope didn't just become a difficult choice but a prerequisite for many if they wanted to move on. And that is what they did; they hoped and they dared to smile for a better future. In the days that followed the first earthquake, I often found myself questioning whether hope was possible, whether we could ever smile again. I asked the same question to people around me. In conversations with them and in their actions I saw the resilience; I saw us all rise again. This collection is a testimony to that hope, not so much to what we lost but to who we are in the wake of that loss.

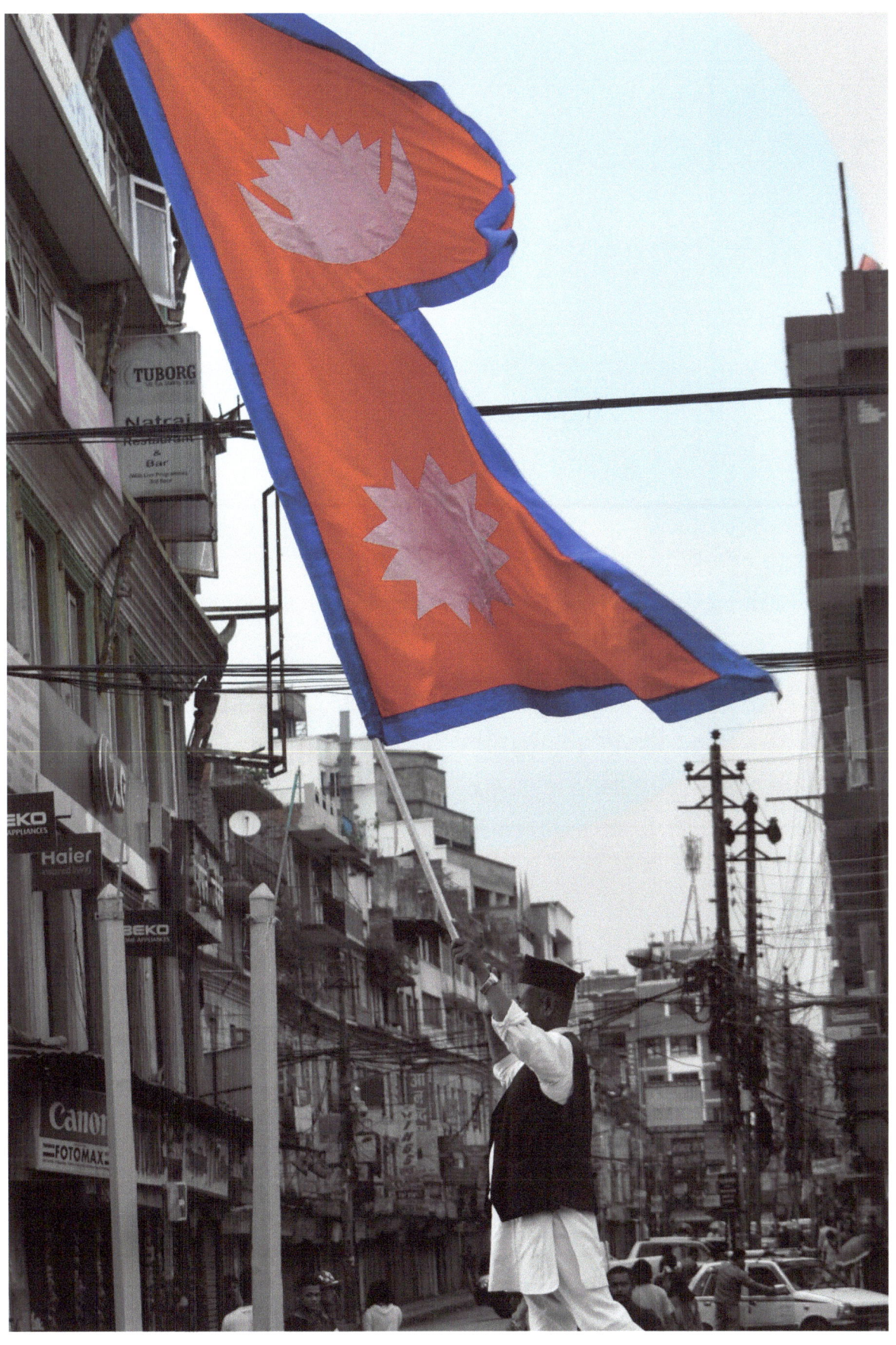

Fragile Home, Humble Smile

A woman welcomed us with a smile from inside her kitchen in a house that was damaged from the devastation. The couple showed us their home and were in a dilemma about whether to renovate or to rebuild the house. We updated them on what's going on in Kathmandu and the places we visited after the earthquake. In no time she offered us a warm cup of tea before we left.

Lele, Lalitpur
18 May 2015

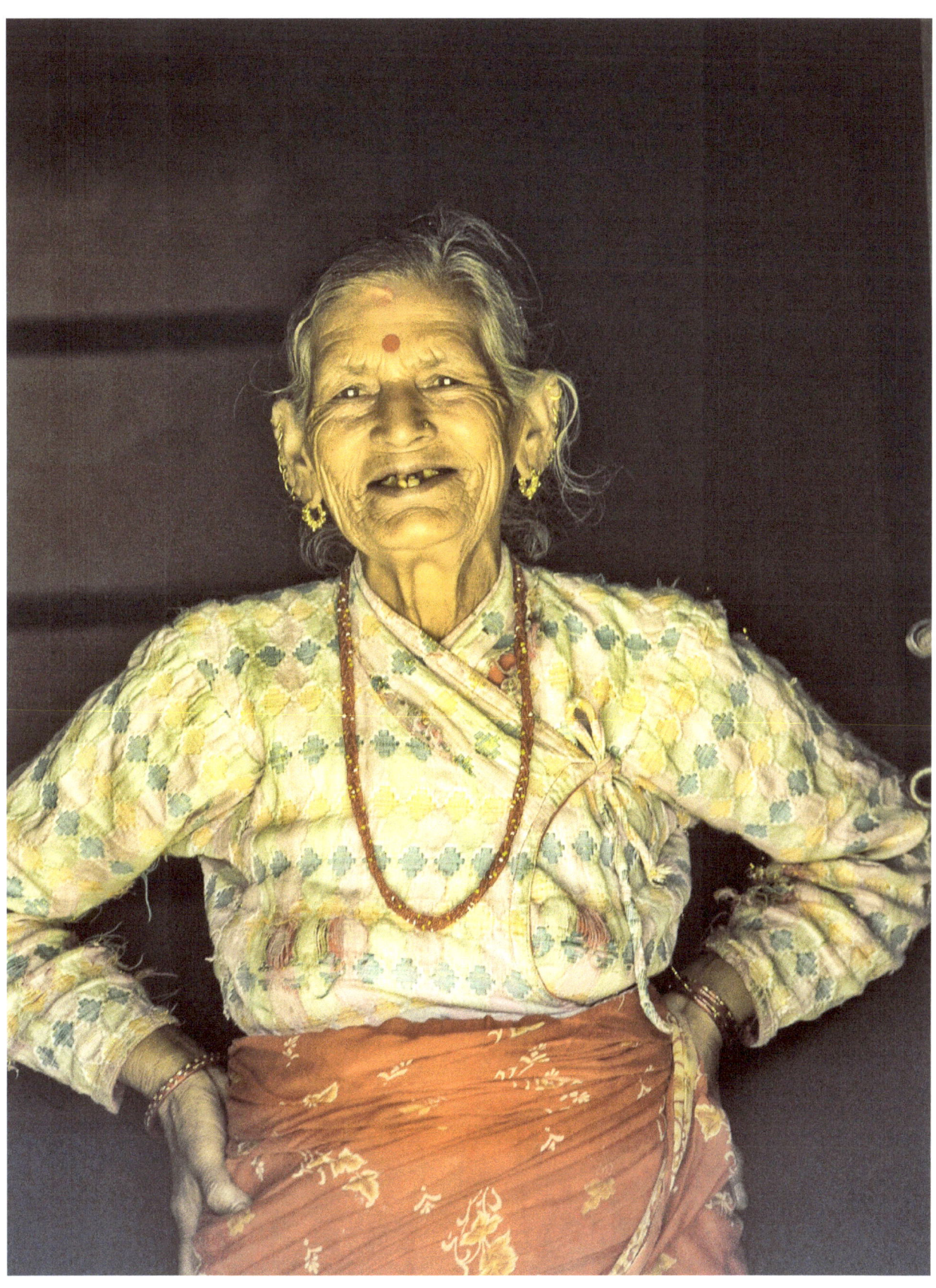

Back to School

Sandesh Singar, from a school in Ikudole, smiles from the temporary learning centre. Thousands of students are continuing their studies in such centres after the earthquake.

Ikudole, Lalitpur
3 February 2016

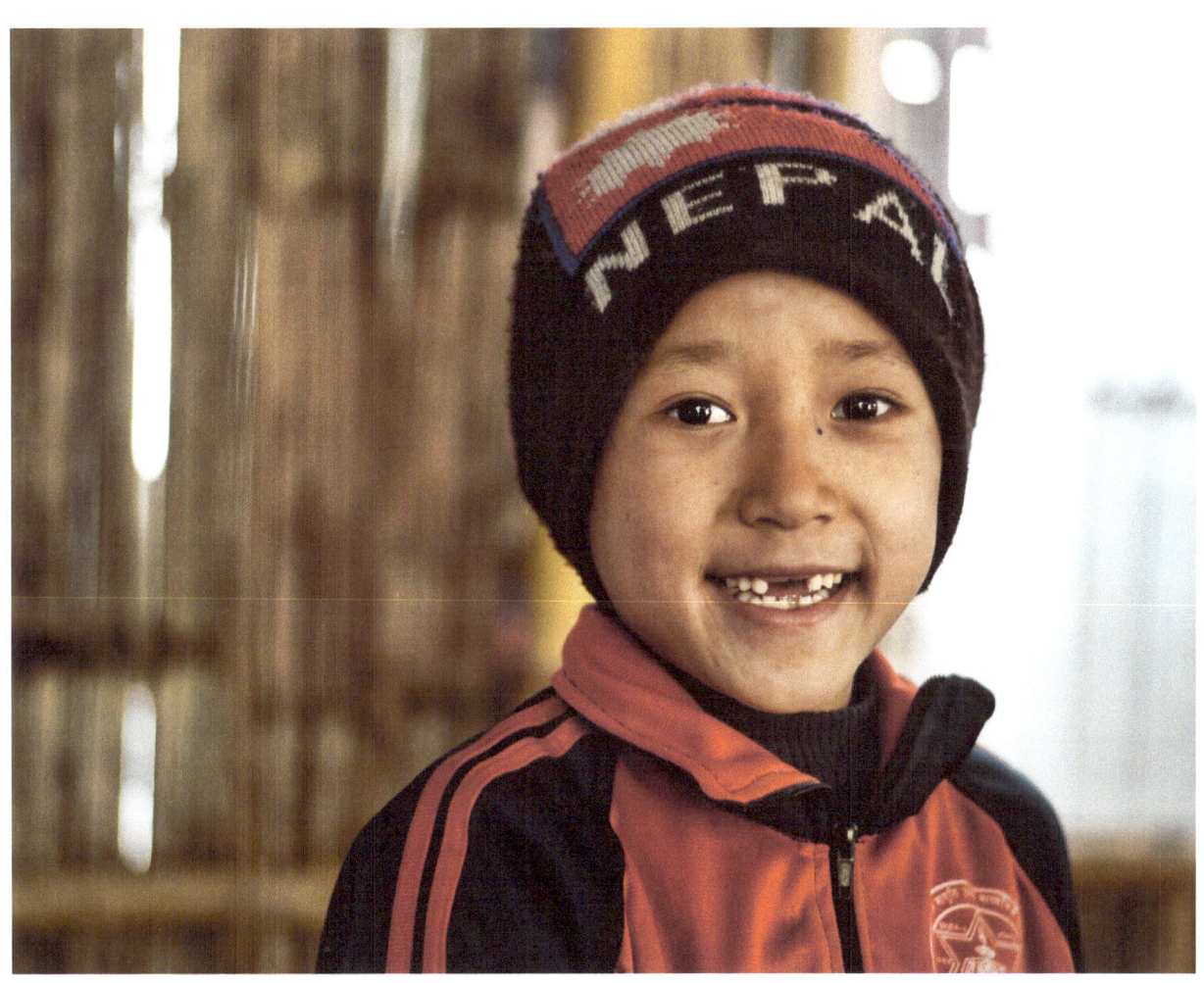

Up in the Himalayas

A little sister is trying her best to make her younger brother happy. When asked if she goes to school, her answer was, "No." When we asked the family why, they simply didn't have any answer. Thousands of students are reported to have abandoned school after the earthquake. This is even more the case in the remote locations that were damaged.

Graham, Rasuwa
31 December 2015

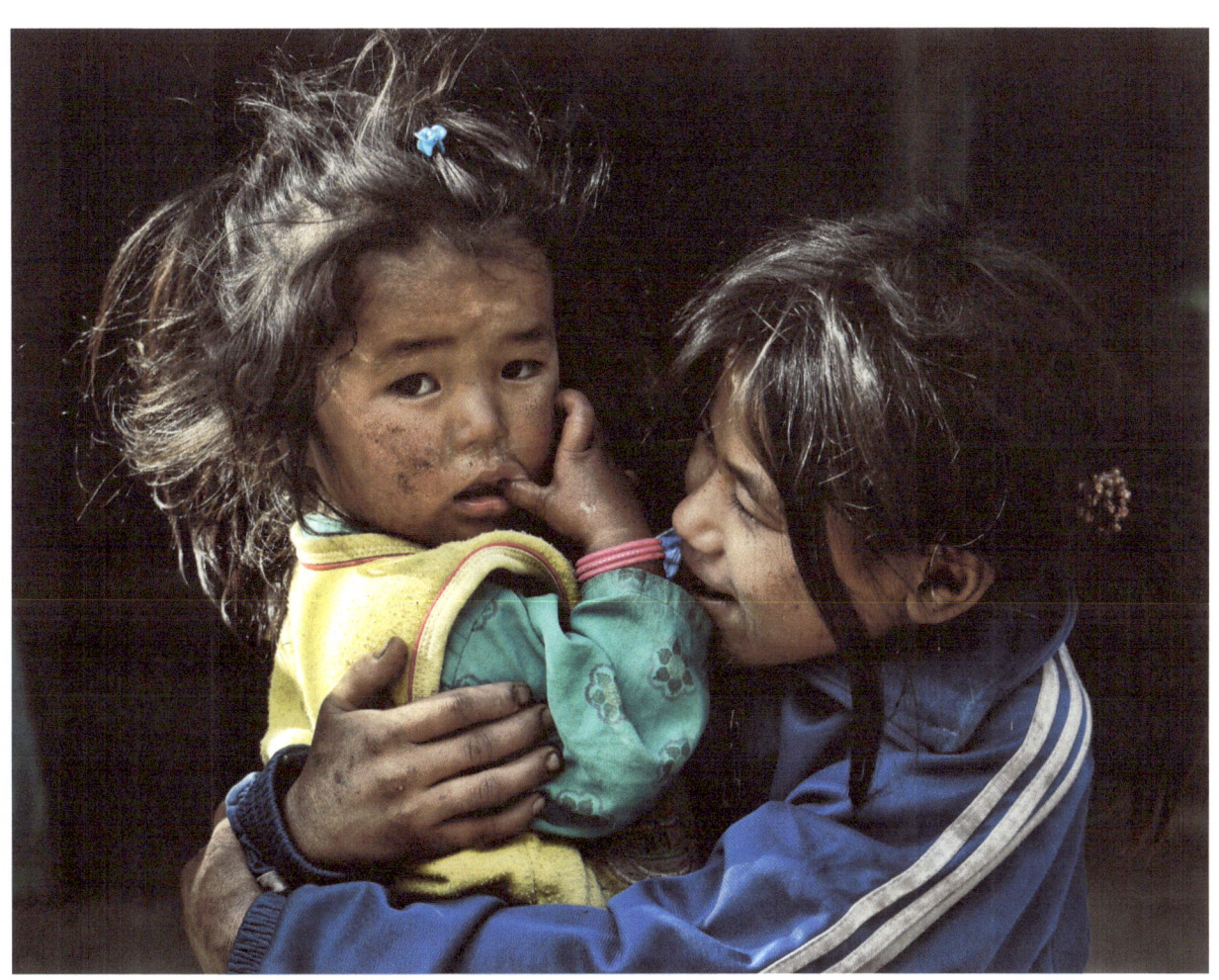

Dhading Smiles

An elderly man in Chhatredeurali, Dhading smiles after receiving a bundle of corrugated galvanised ironsheet as an emergency relief distributed by a volunteer group. His village is among the worst affected in Dhading, where fifty people have lost their lives and thousands of others were injured. Almost all the houses are severely damaged from the earthquake.

Chhatredeurali, Dhading
18 June 2015

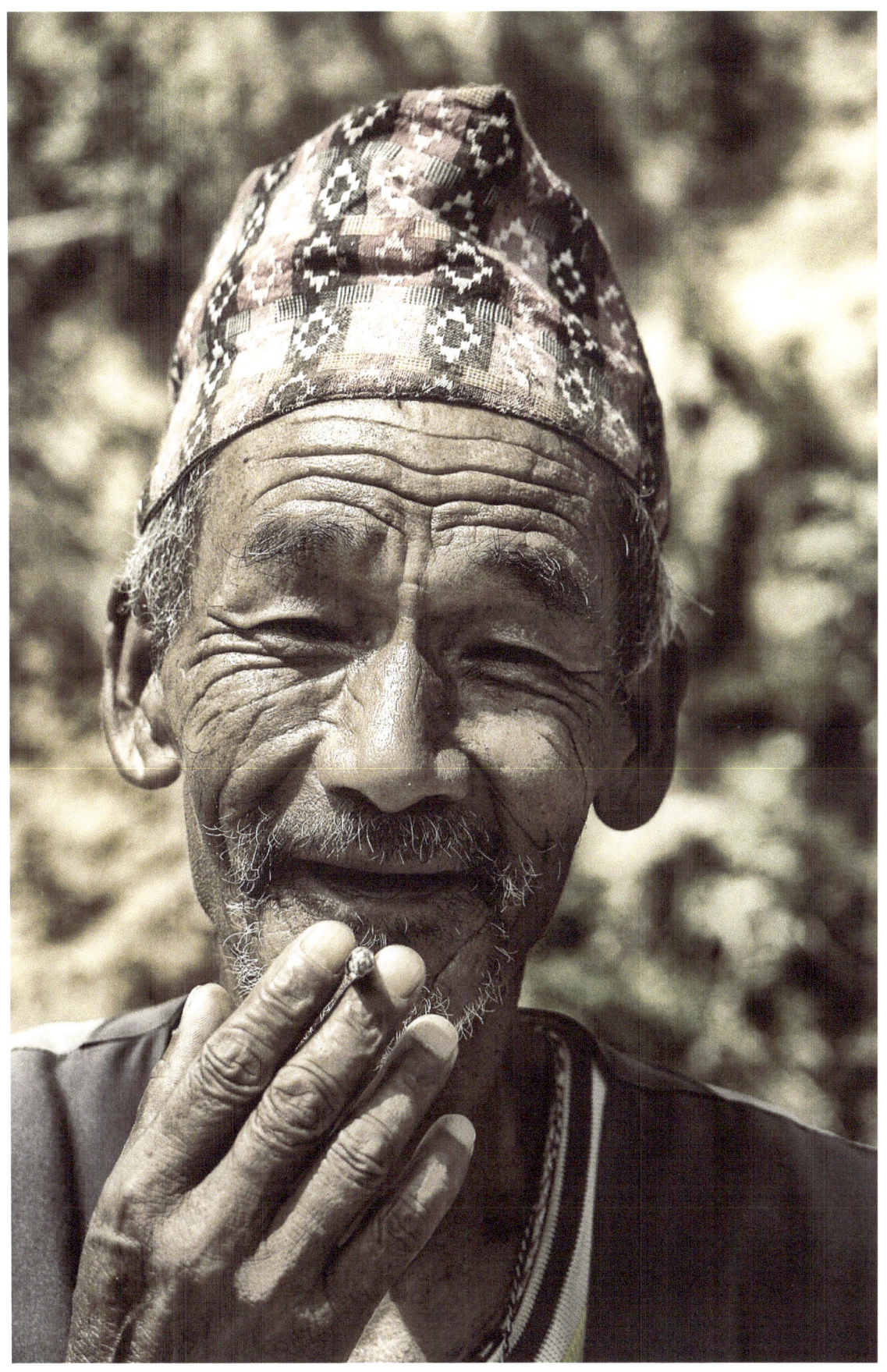

Lady in a Red Scarf

A lady is seen smiling in a local street market near Durbar Square, Kathmandu. People were seen talking about the traumatic experience they had during the earthquake and how they managed to save their lives. The local street market near the world heritage sight is popular amongst the middle class populations in Kathmandu as things are sold at affordable prices.

Kathmandu
12 June 2015

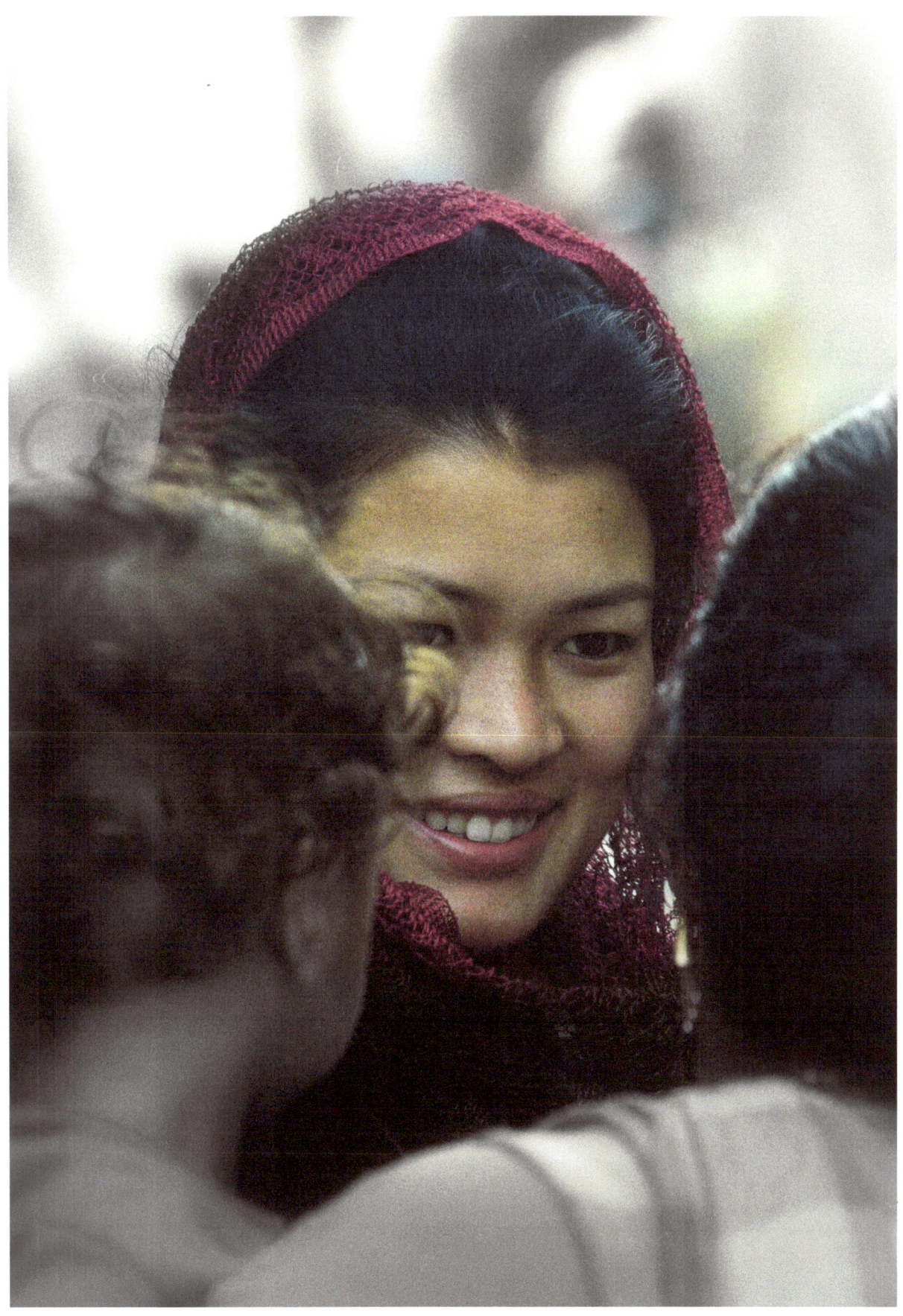

Nepal Gets a New Constitution

Street celebration as seen around Tudikhel, Kathmandu to welcome the much anticipated new Constitution of Nepal. The earthquake not only left tragedy and sufferings, but also brought the major political stakeholders together to promulgate the constitution. The constitution is welcomed mostly in hilly and Himalayan regions, but the situation in the southern plains turned worse with dissatisfaction from the political groups there.

Kathmandu
21 September 2015

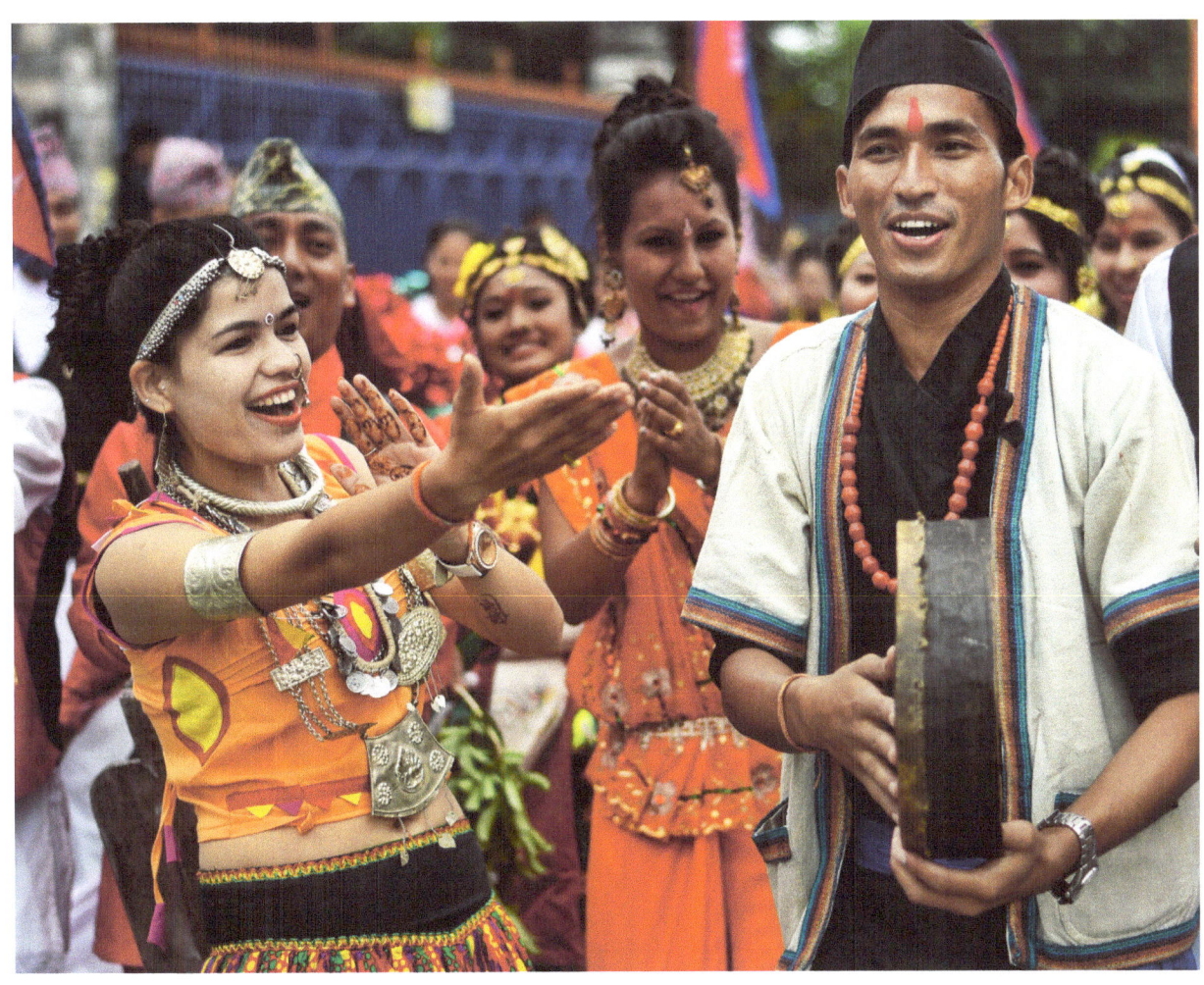

Unity in Diversity

Diverse ethnic communities in their traditional attires celebrate the new Constitution in Nepal. Nepal is a home to over one hundred ethnic groups. The political development had polarized various groups, however the devastation gave a space for all to come together and work for humanity.

Kathmandu
21 September 2015

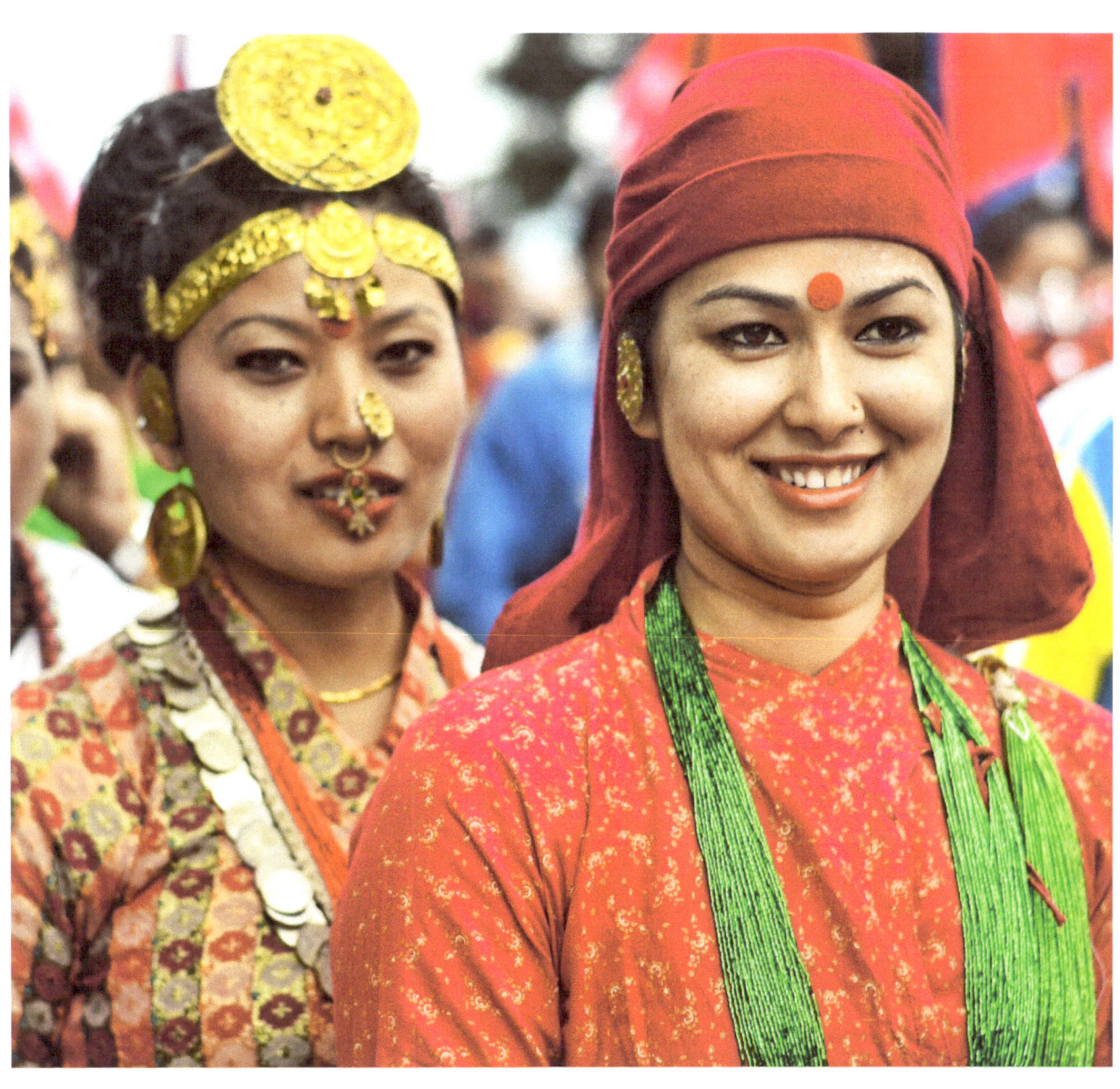

The Legacy of Kathmandu

Nati Maharjan from Kathmandu believes that the rebuilding of world heritage sites will begin soon, so that the upcoming generations will see the legacy of their forefathers.

Kathmandu

2 February 2016

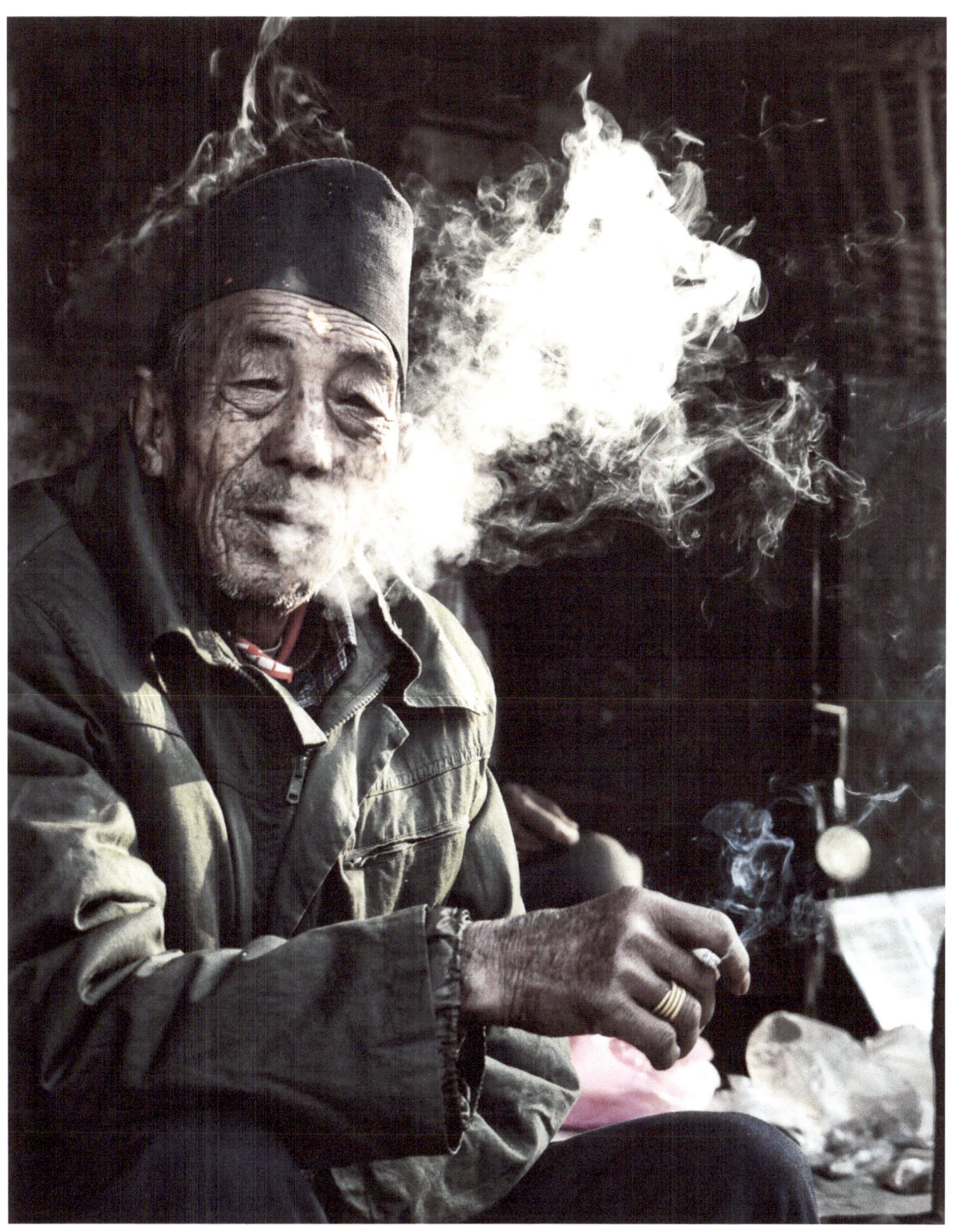

Wrinkle Stories

A woman from the Tamang community in Chhatredeurali, Dhading walked hours to receive relief materials. A significant number of people from the Tamang ethnic group reside in all fourteen of the worst affected districts of Nepal.

Chhatredeurali, Dhading
8 July 2015

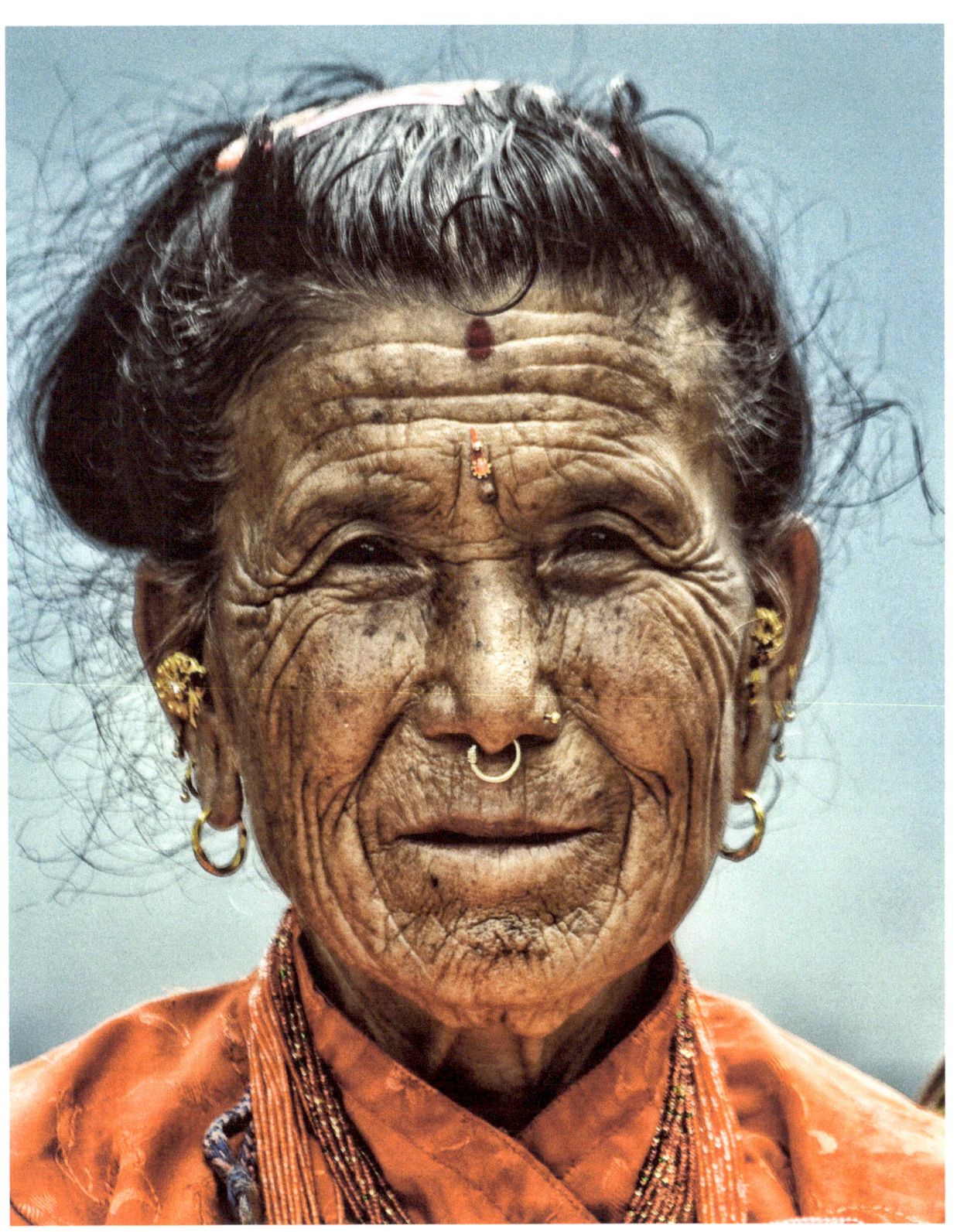

Street Smiles Here in Kathmandu

An elderly woman who runs a street shop in Asan, Kathmandu smiles with her customer.

Asan, Kathmandu
11 November 2015

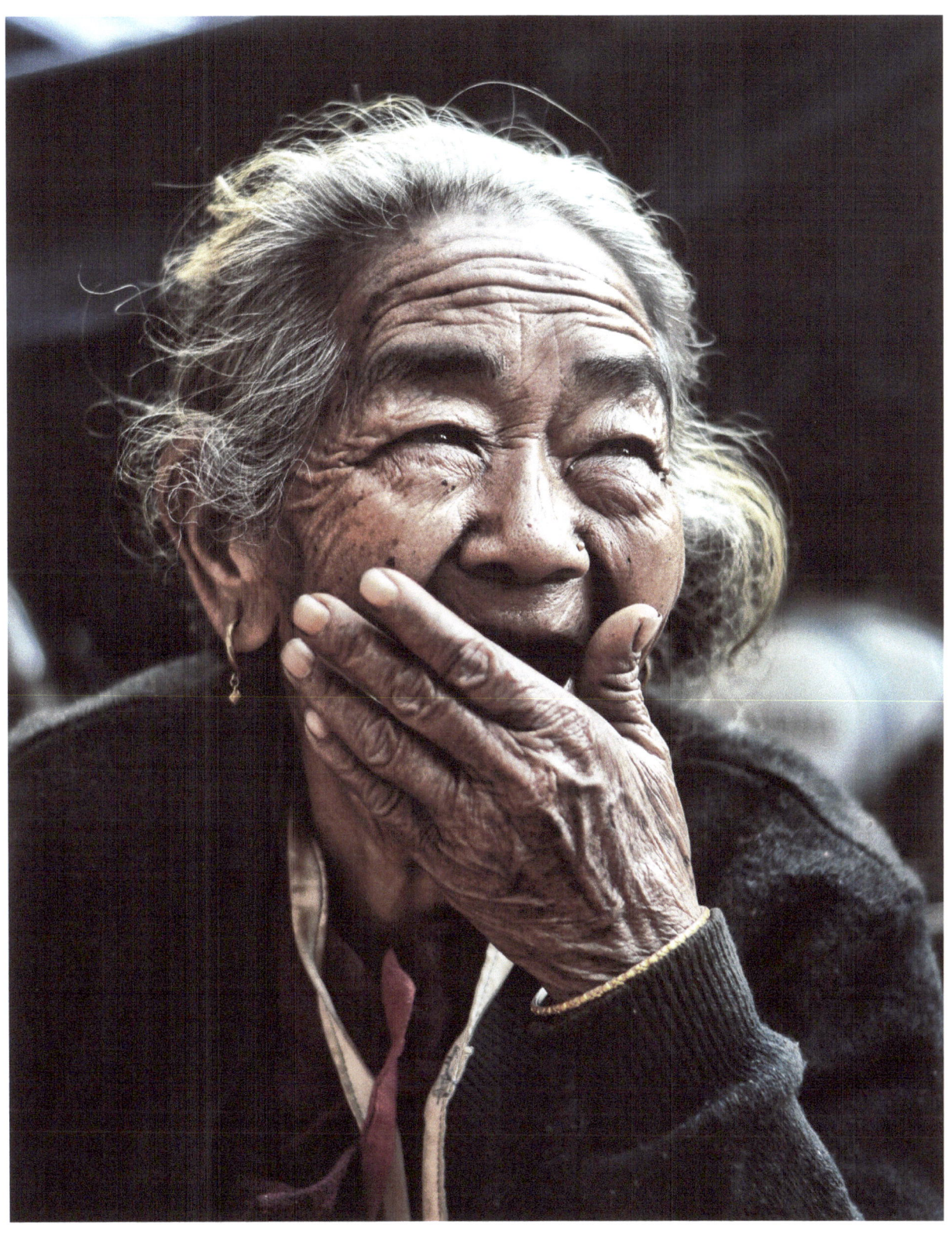

School Resumes

In Sindhupalchowk, after twenty days school resumes in safe spaces amidst damaged buildings. Because of frequent aftershocks, parents were afraid to keep their children at home in the community where any remaining building could fall at any time. So parents found it safe to send their children to school where teachers could engage them throughout the day.

Thumki, Sindhupalchowk
16 June 2015

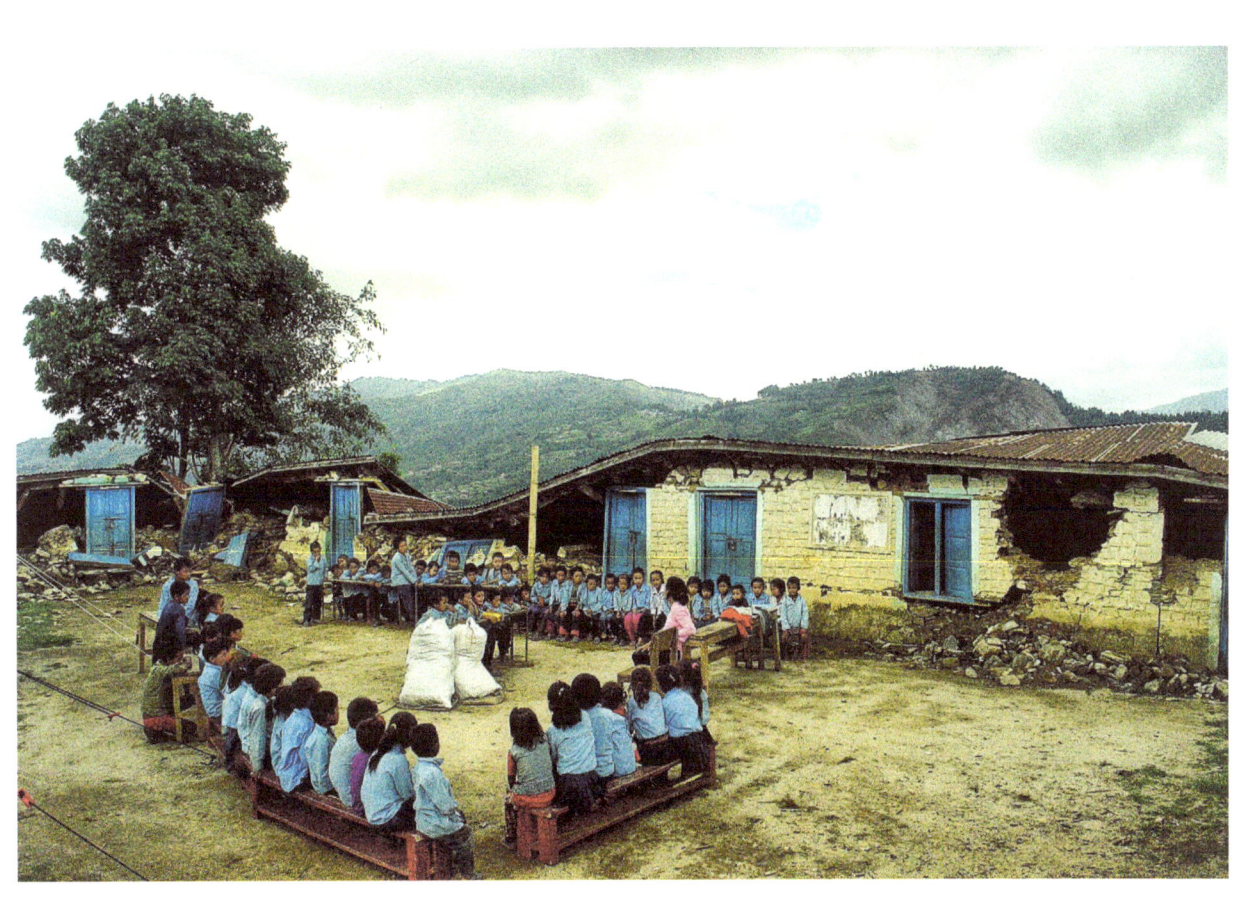

Resilience

Kalpana Giri, a mother of four children from Gaikhura, Ramechhap, smiles outside of her small temporary cottage. Their collapsed building, which is behind the cottage, is not cleared.

Gaikhura, Ramechhap
19 November 2015

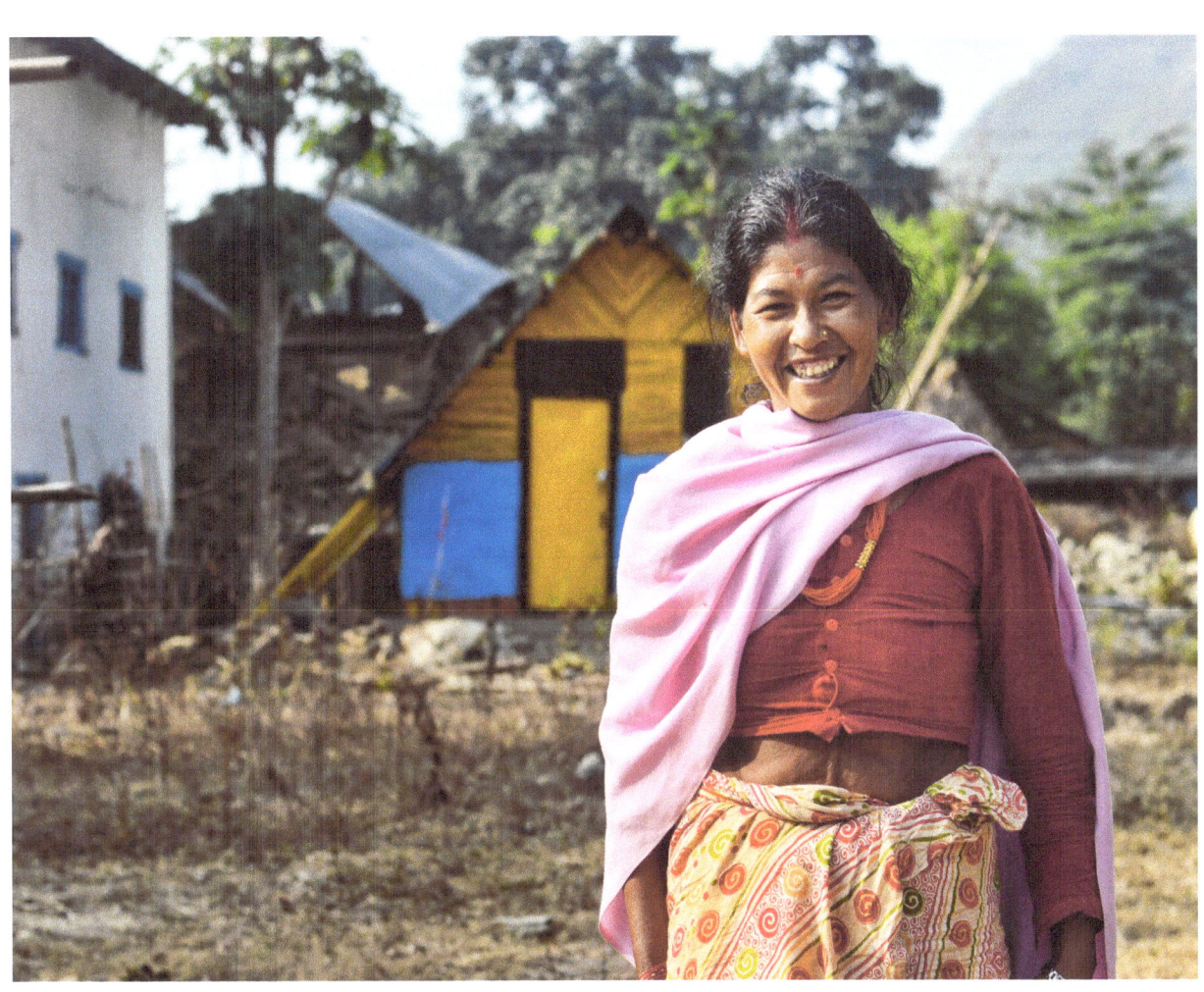

Some Smiles Have Tears in Them

A child crying with his mother all of a sudden smiles for the camera. He still has tears in his eyes.

Dhunche, Rasuwa
31 December 2015

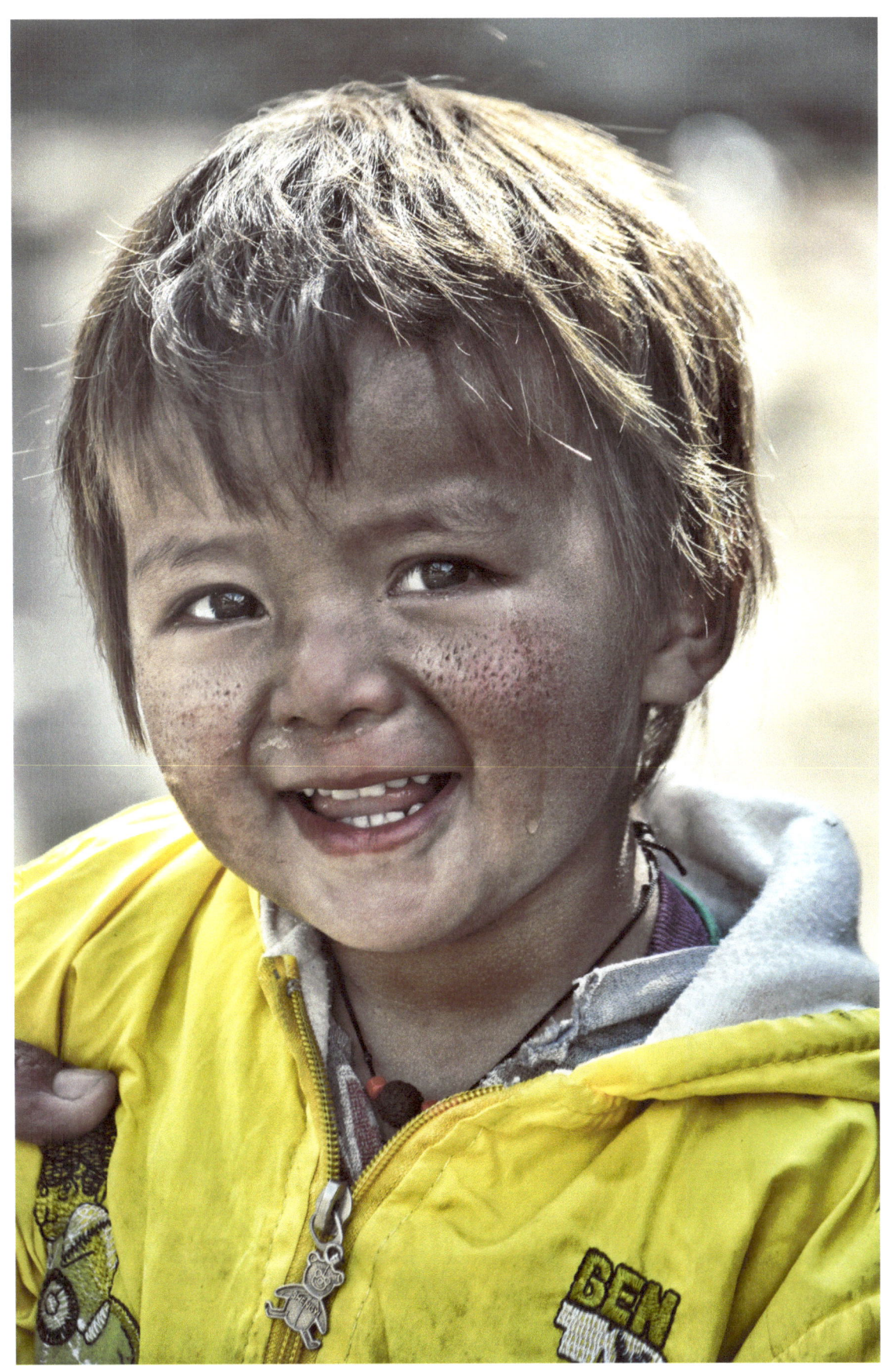

A Long Wait

An elderly woman is waiting her turn for the relief materials that were being provided by an NGO in Dhading.

,

Dhading
8 July 2015

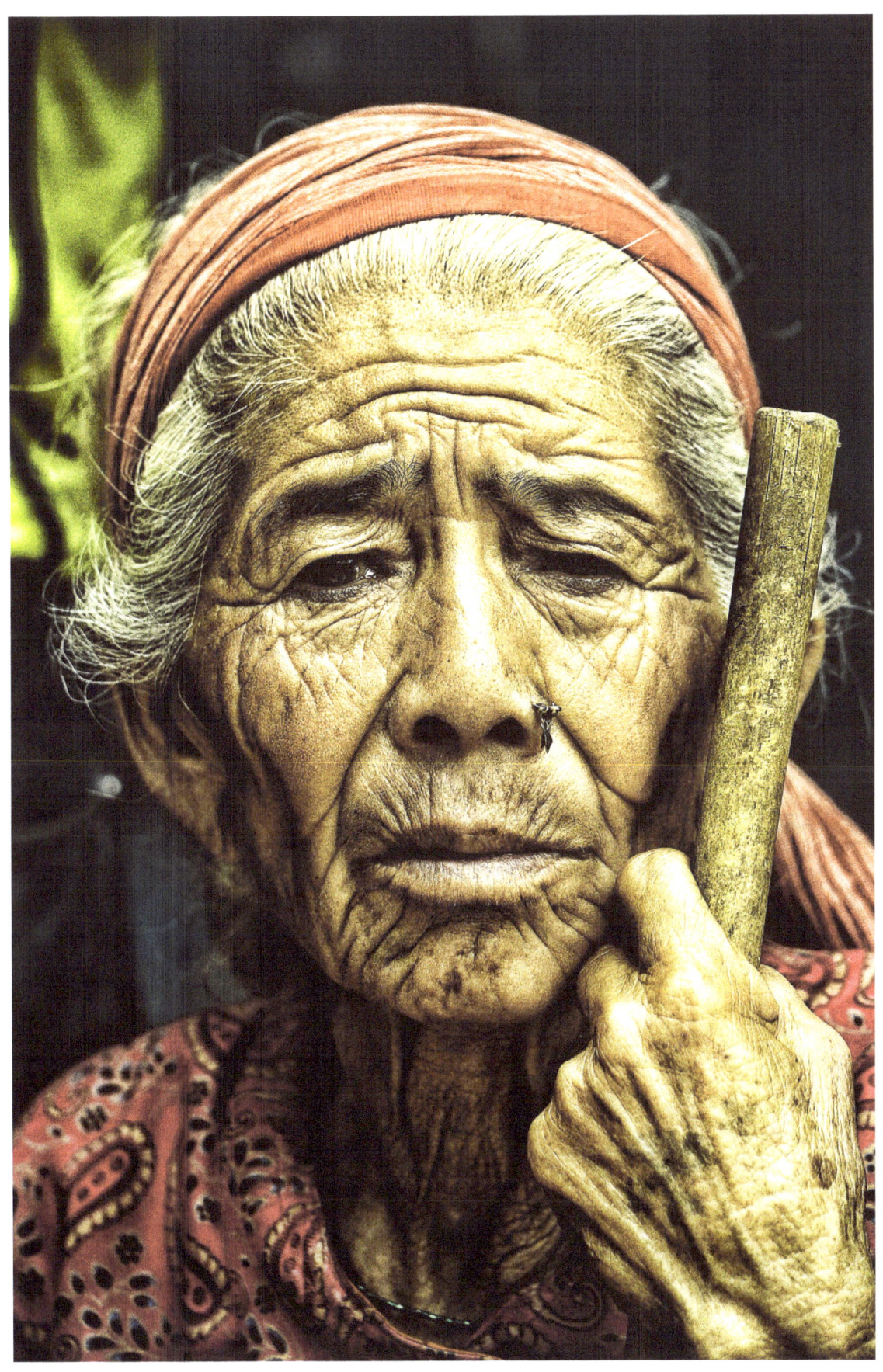

Little Lady with a Smile

A fifth grader from Sindhupalchowk rests in the shade while her parents are busy working to reconstruct the school.

Thulopakhar, Sindhupalchowk
3 June 2015

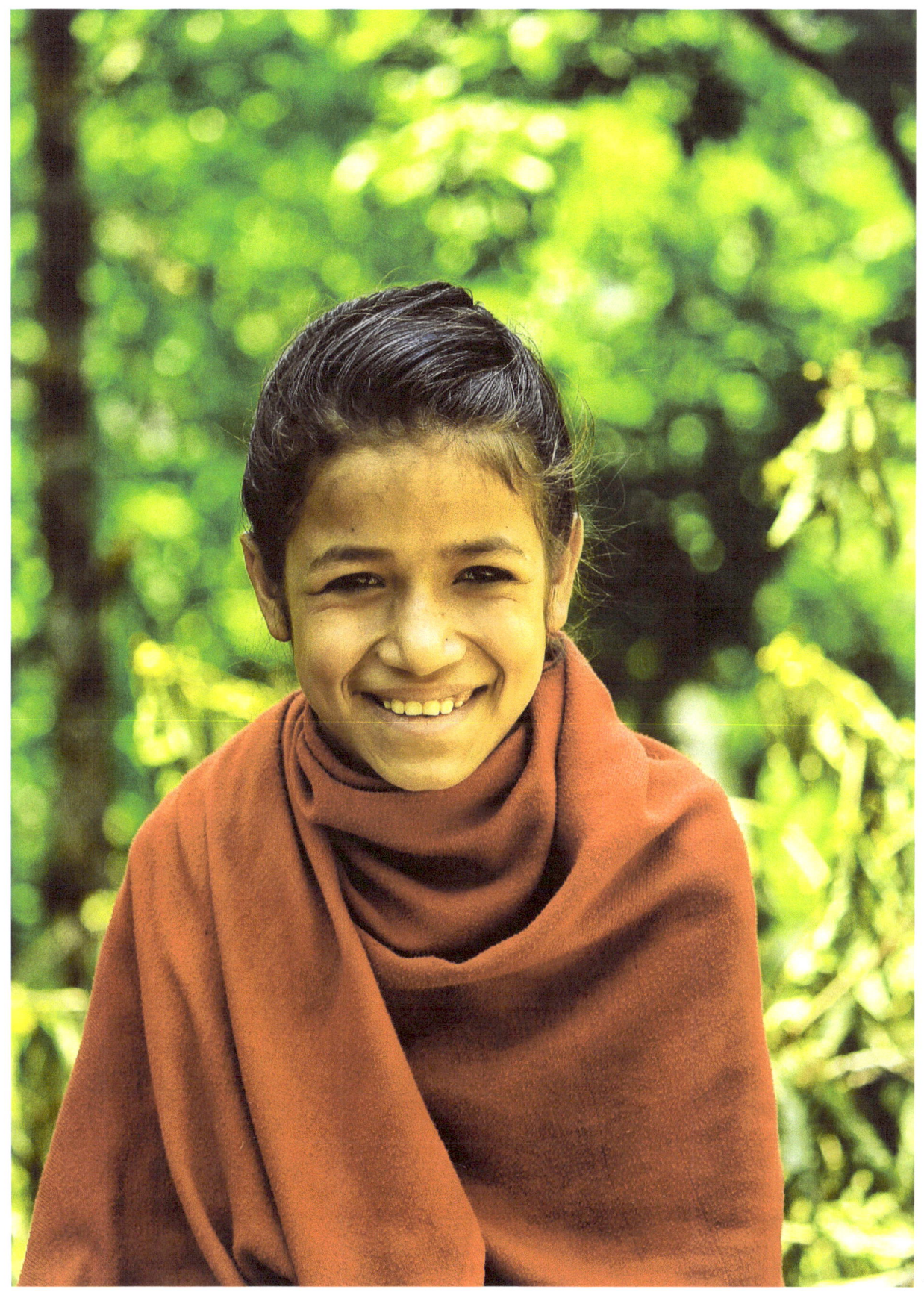

Daily Life Continues

A woman in Ikudol, Lalitpur is in her buffalo shed. Selling milk in the city is a major source of income for her and the local communities.

Ikudol, Lalitpur
3 February 2016

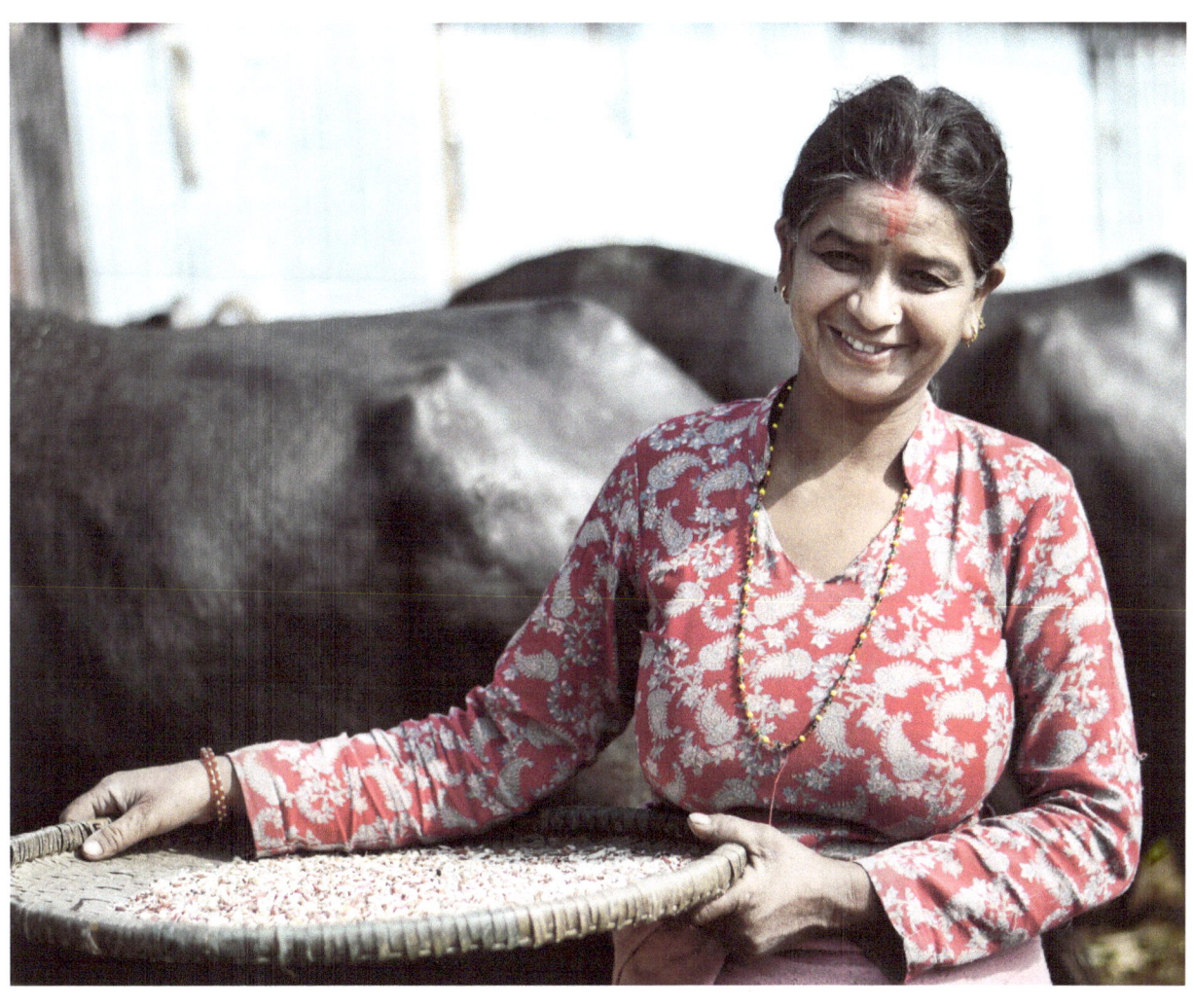

Smile from the Hollow Classroom

Sarita Bhandari is with her friends in their collapsed school in Sindhupalchowk. The girls came to school to receive the educational materials that were distributed by an organization called "Moving-Mountains."

Sindhupalchowk
3 June 2015

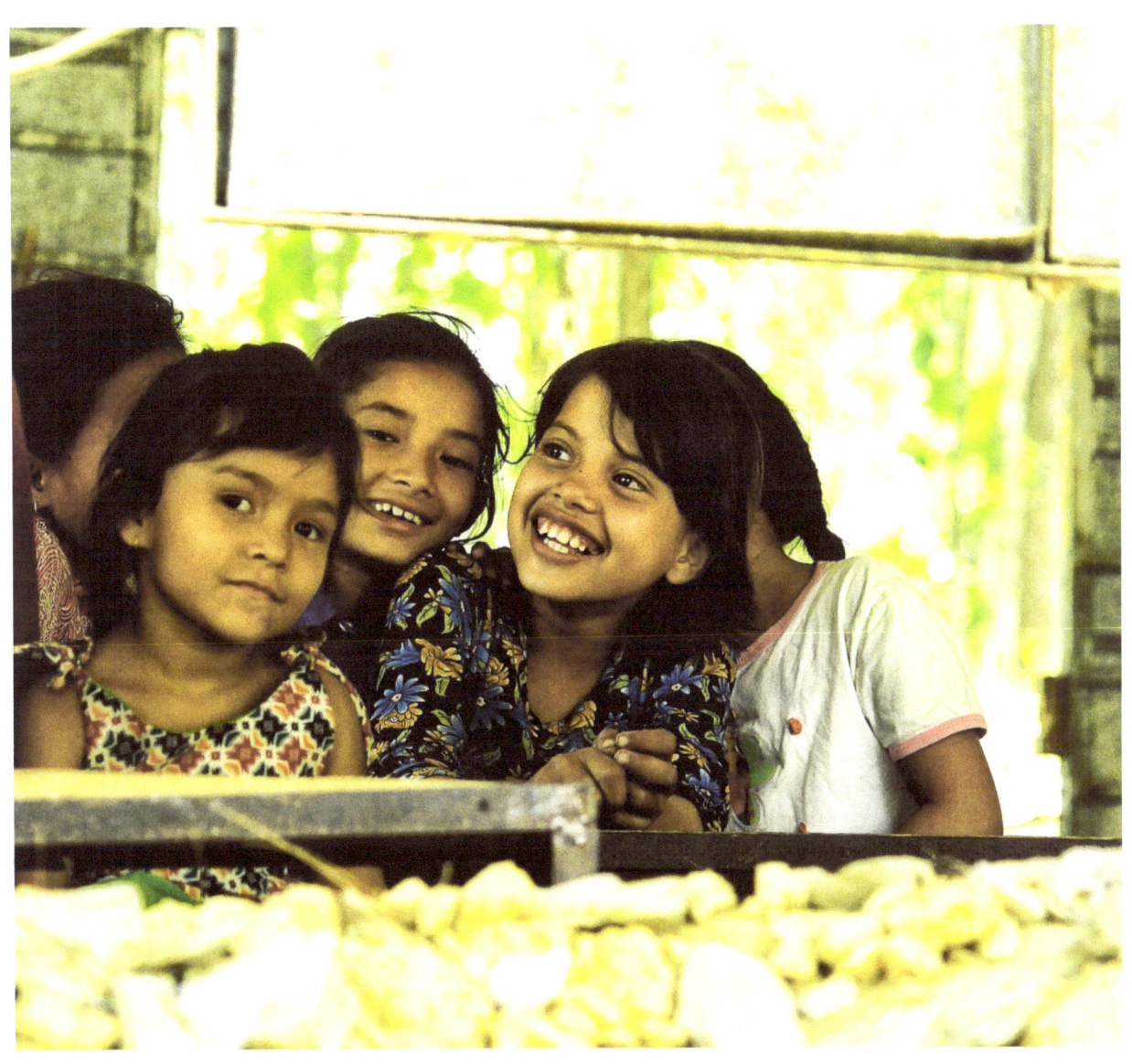

Early Morning Smile

An elderly man smiles in Kathmandu's Durbar Square. After the collapse, Durbar Square and the premises became the safe spaces for locals living nearby.

Kathmandu
12 June 2015

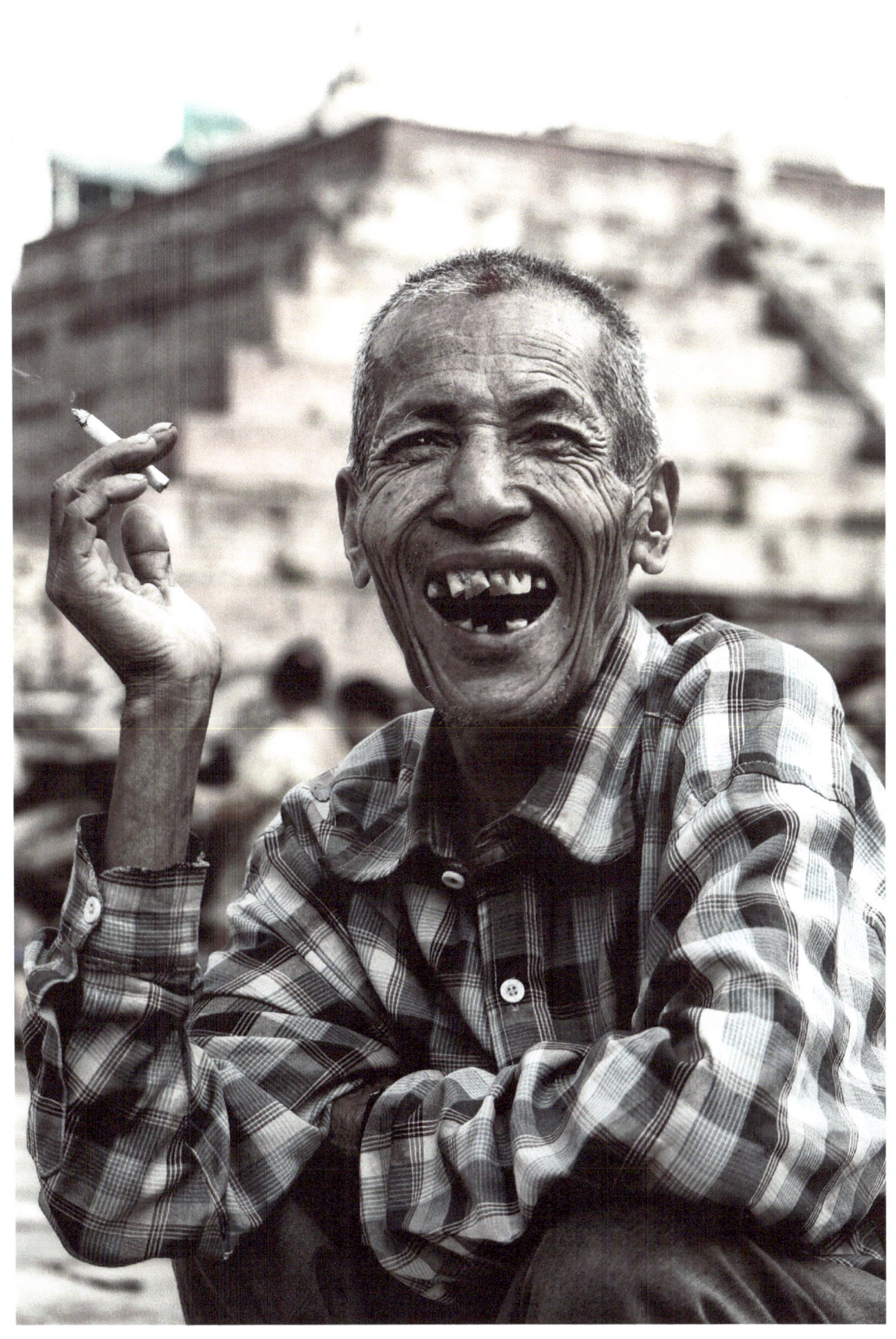

Kavrepalanchowk Smiles

This powerful smile comes from Kavrepalanchowk. I met him in a local grocery shop in Dolalghat. When I asked permission to take a picture, he gave a flawless smile.

Kavrepalanchowk
3 June 2015

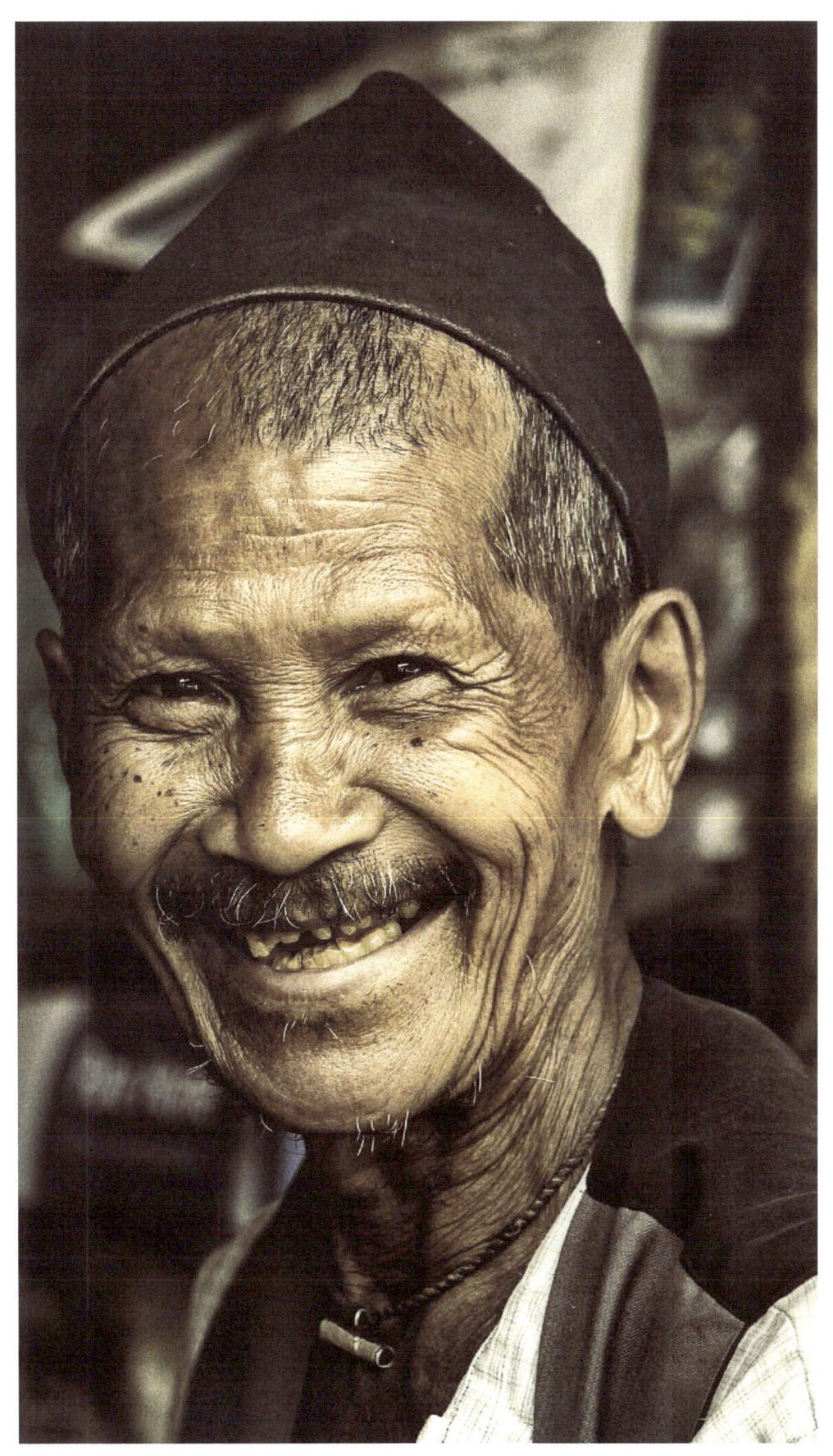

A Break from Hard Field Work

"It's useless to recall the incidents from the earthquakes; now we have to move on. In a few weeks I will be harvesting wheat and will prepare the field for paddy if it rains early this time."

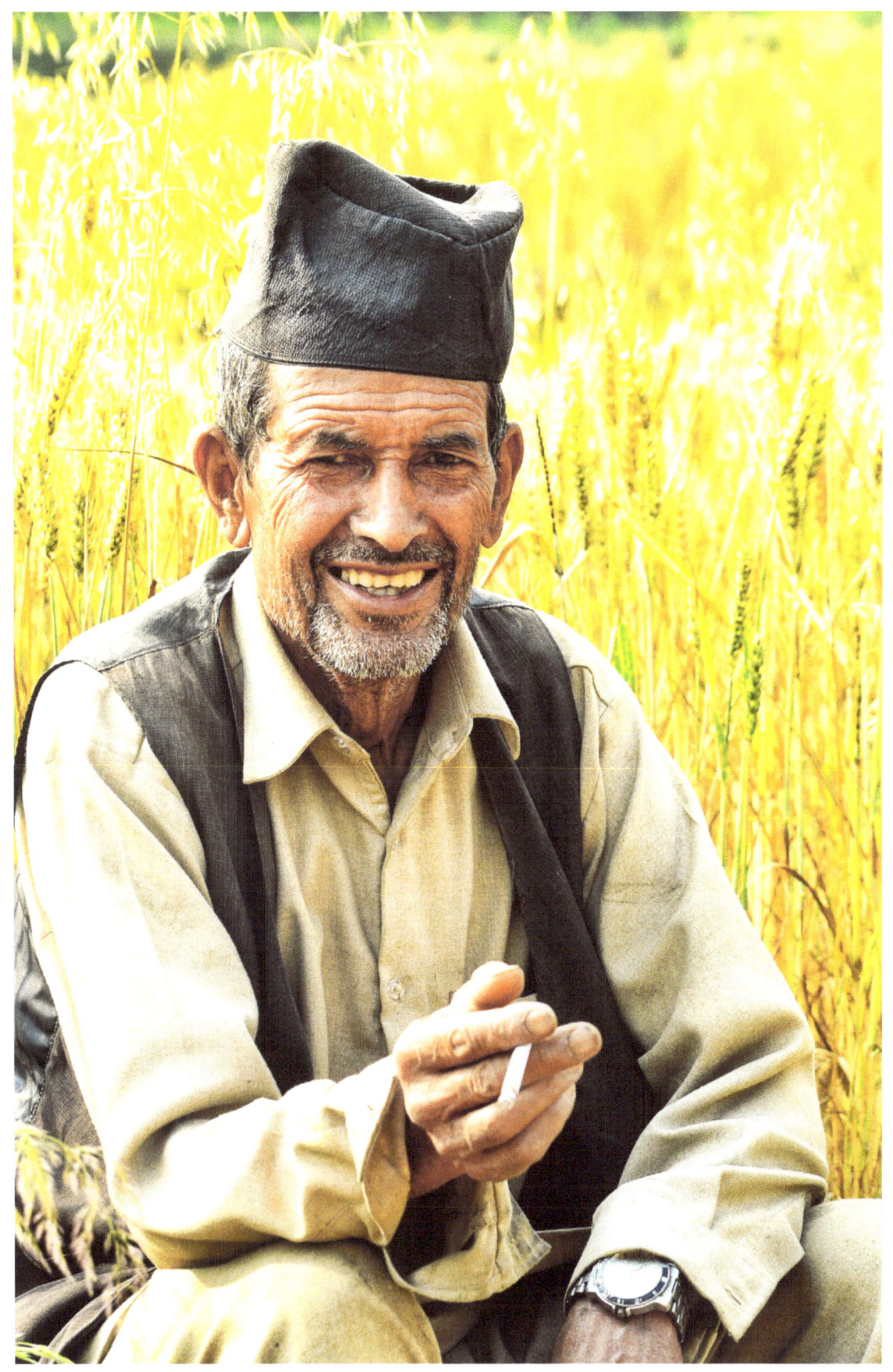

Father's Love

"My daughter gets lost and remembers the devastation and death that she saw through her eyes. We have not left her alone lately. We hope our village and family will recover soon."

Thulopakhar, Sindhupchowk
3 June 2015

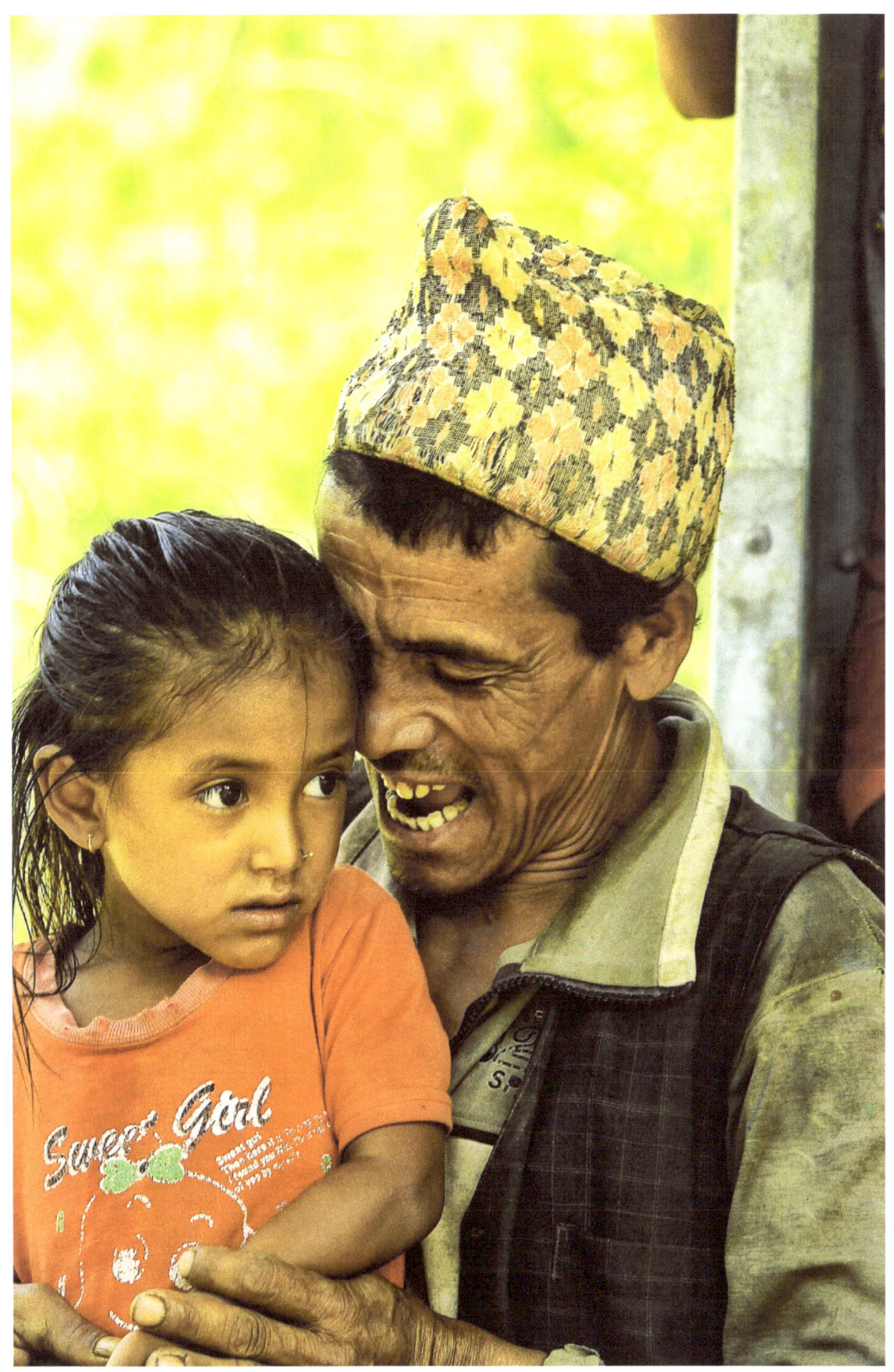

Wrinkle Story

"Age should not have its face lifted, but it should rather teach the world to admire wrinkles as the etchings of experience and the firm line of character."
    — Clarence Day

Dhading
8 July 2015

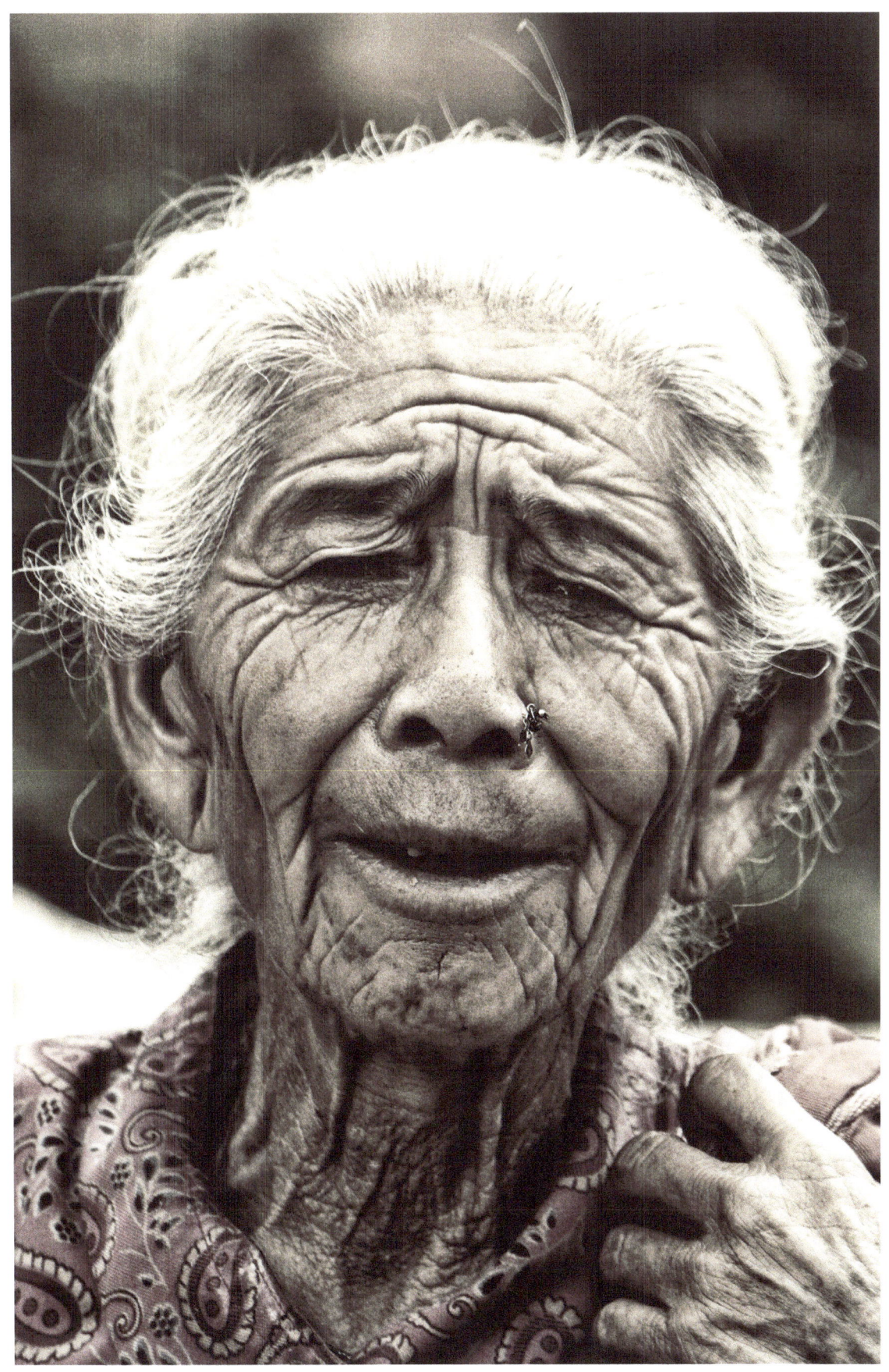

Earthquake Took Away Something, Not Everything

"The earthquake took away our home but not our lands. Working hard there heals our pains."

Bhotechaur, Sindhupalchowk
23 June 2015

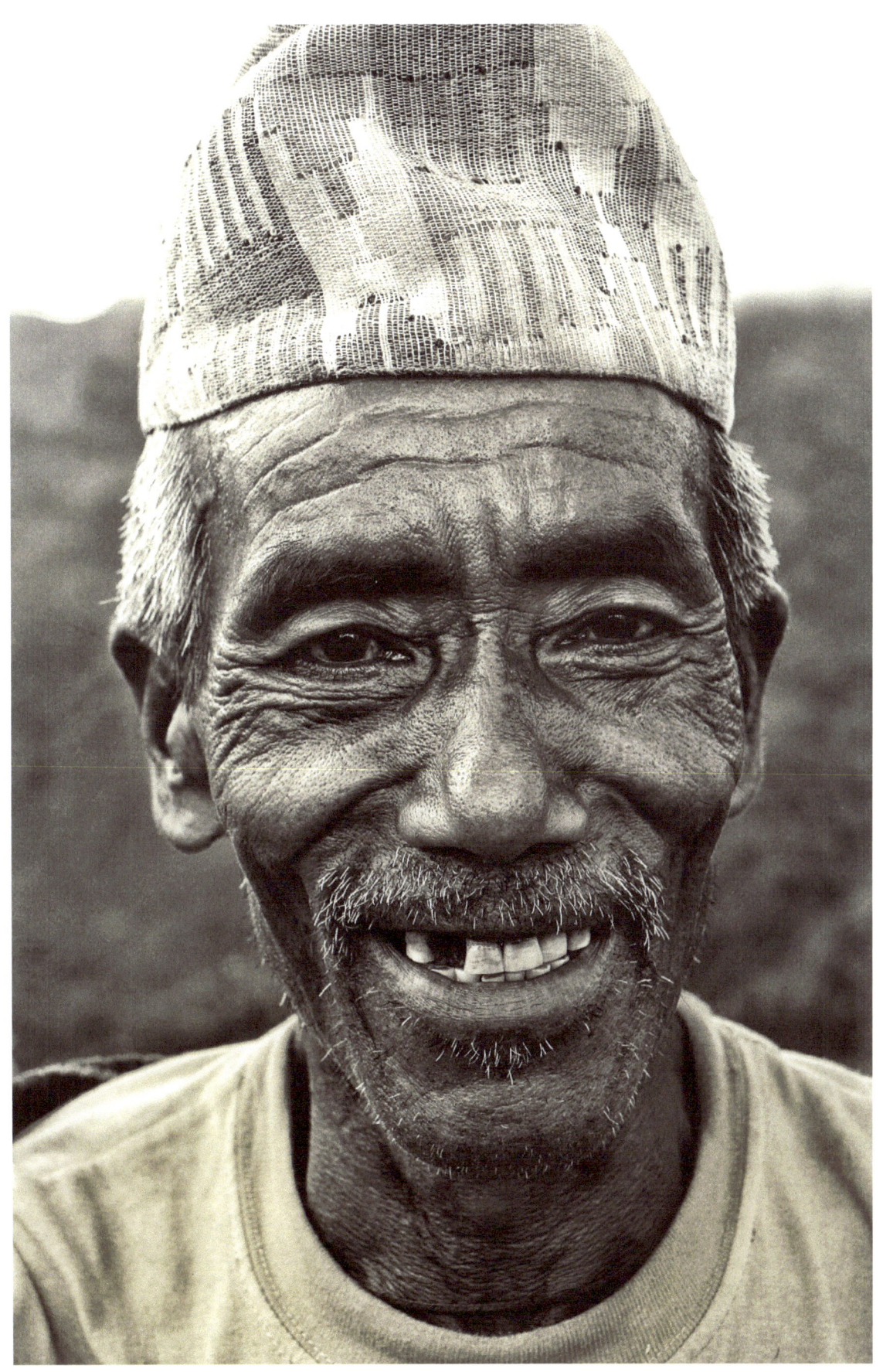

Wary Eyes

It was not only resilience and smiles that were observed. There was also pain, frustration and uncertainty. I could see them in their eyes.

Kathmandu
2 February 2016

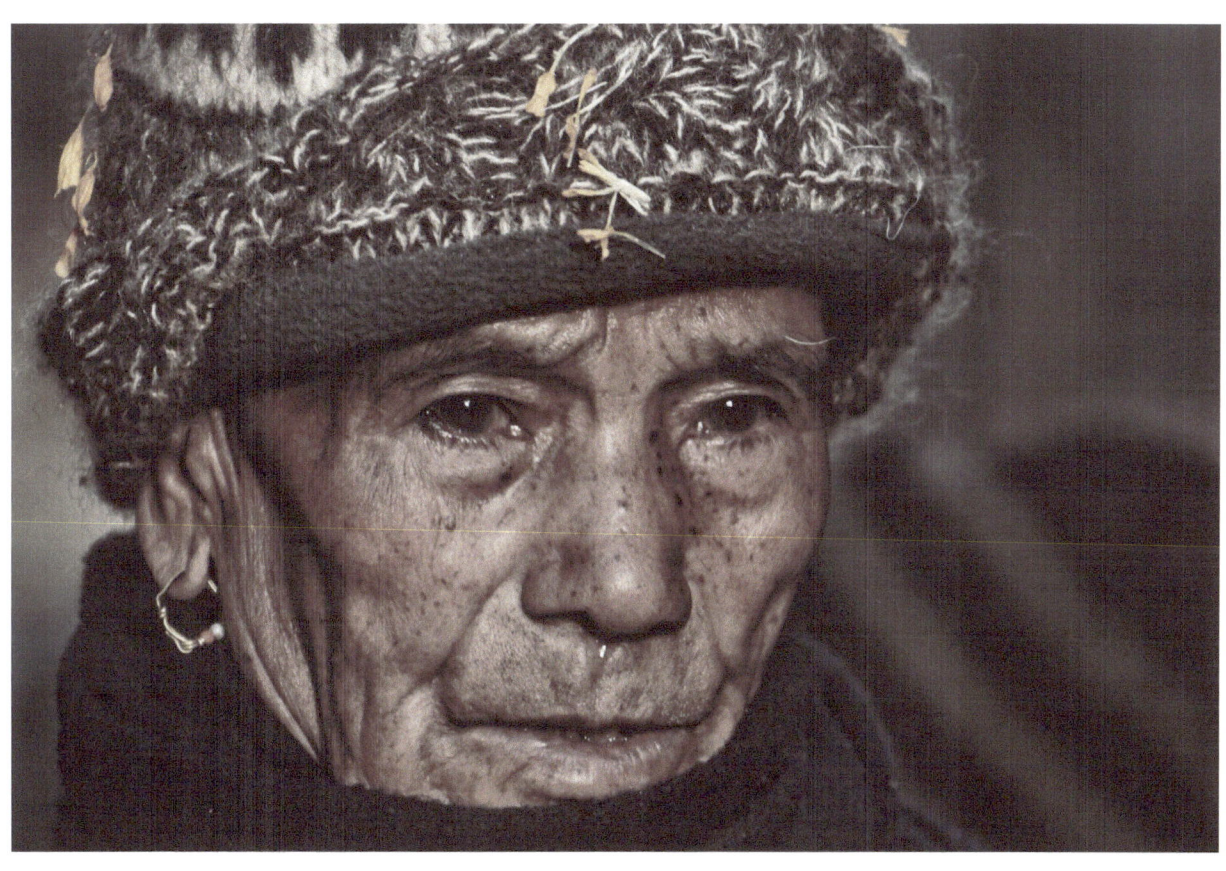

Nepal Smiles Again

"If the world's a veil of tears, smile until rainbows span it."
— Lucy Larco

Sindhupalchowk
8 June 2015

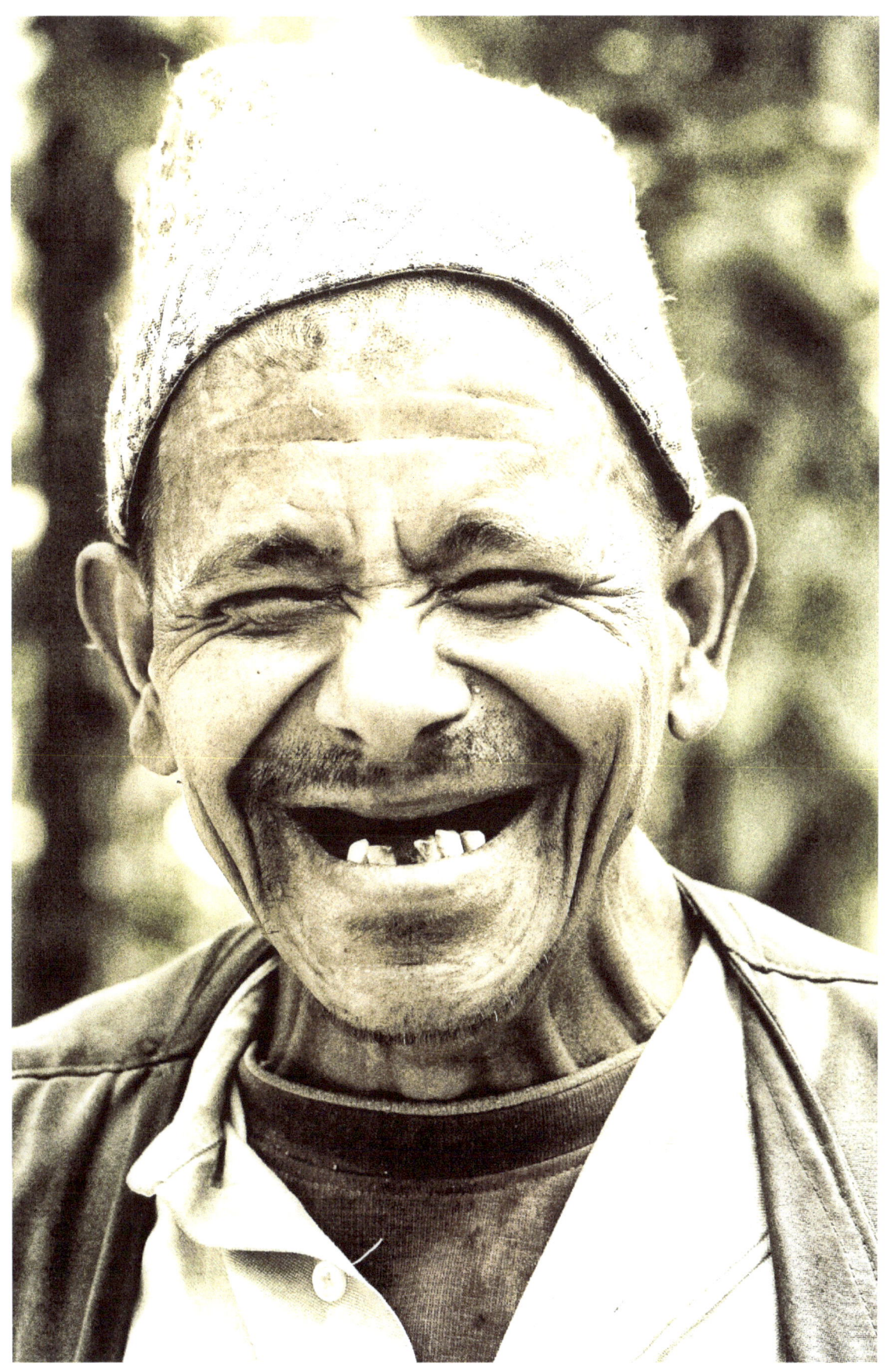

One Year of Road to Recovery

April 25, 2016
Nepal marked a year of
road to recovery from the devastating earthquake.
Prayer goes to all who are
affected by the tragedy.
May around 10,000 departed souls rest in peace.
Nepal Smiles Again.
We will build and recover.

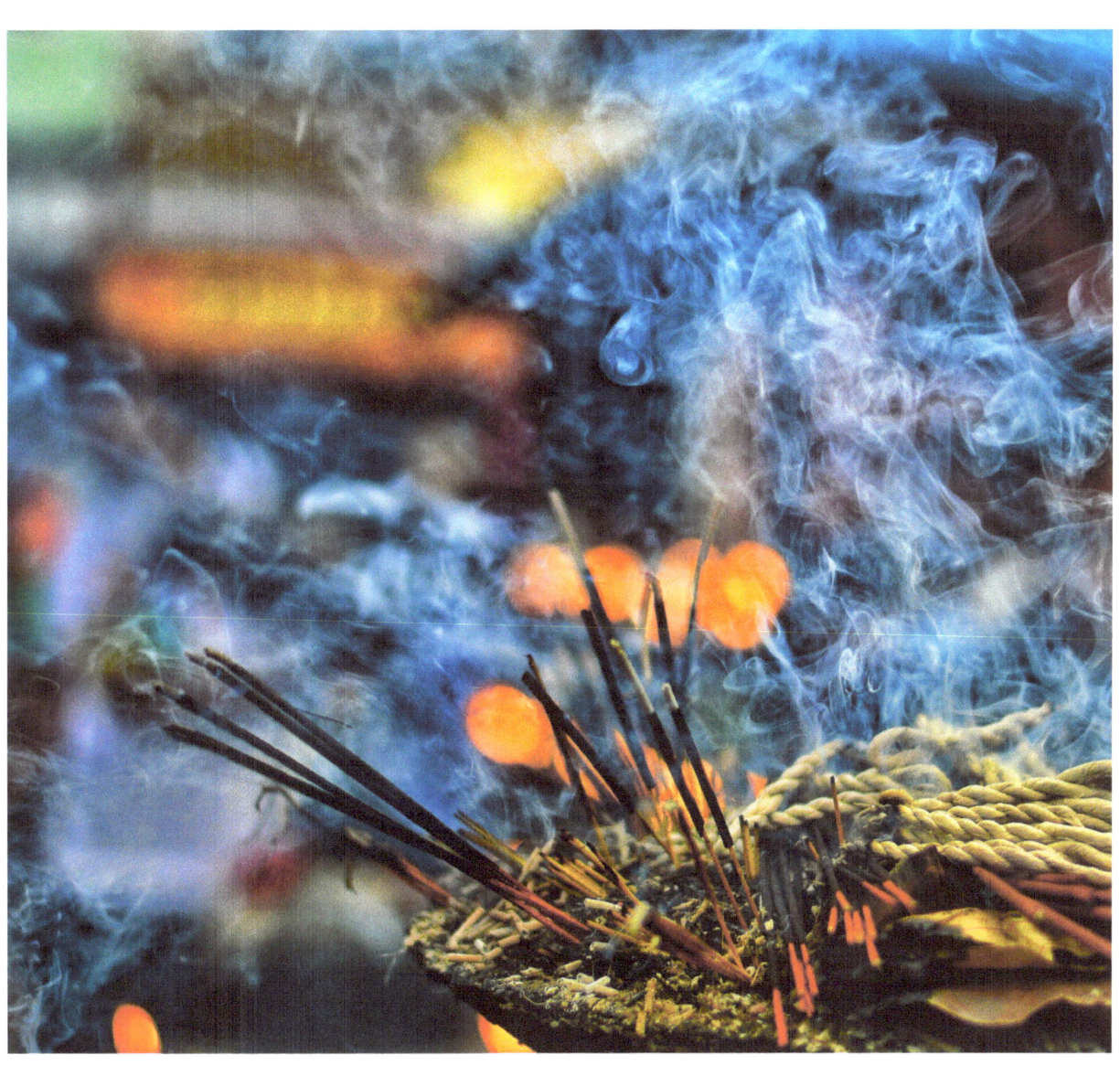

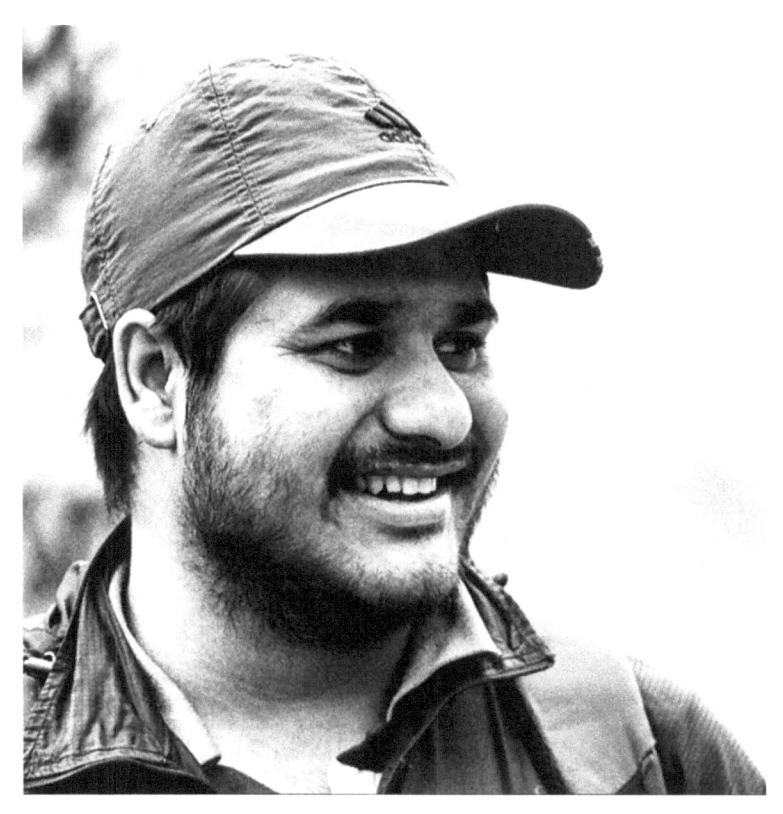

Manoj Pandey is a young peace practitioner and a portrait photography enthusiast from Nepal. He has had extensive experience in dialogue facilitation, mediation, peace-building, and research and development for six years. Mr. Pandey holds a master's degree in Conflict, Peace, and Development Studies from Tribhuvan University, Nepal. He is currently a fellow for a master's degree in Applied Conflict Transformation from the Center for Peace and Conflict Studies with an affiliation with Pannasastra University, Cambodia.

Most of the images and video broadcasts during and after the earthquakes were full of blood, pain, rubble, and deaths. The photographer's individual initiative "Nepal Smiles Again" explores the smiles on the faces of people amidst the pain, sufferings, and frustration.

3 May 2016

Contact information:
Manozpandey.cpds@gmail.com
www.instagram.com/manozpandey
www.facebook.com/manoz.pandey

www.ingramcontent.com/pod-product-compliance
Lightning Source LLC
Chambersburg PA
CBHW050757180526
45159CB00003B/1489